How To Buy Your First Home Or
Investment Property With

Carleton H. Sheets™

No Down Payment™

Volume 2:

Becoming A Real Estate Investor

STEP-BY-STEP MANUAL
Sixth Edition, Revised And Expanded

The Professional Education Institute
www.CarletonSheets.com

This course is designed to provide accurate and authoritative information regarding the subject matter covered. The author and publisher are not engaged in rendering legal, accounting or other professional services to any person. If legal advice and/or other expert assistance is required, the service of a competent professional should be sought.

It is advised that any document you use from this book be approved by your local attorney who knows your particular local laws.

Published by The Professional Education Institute
© 1985-2005
The Professional Education Institute
All Rights Reserved
Printed in the United States of America

The Carleton H. Sheets™ *No Down Payment*™ course of The Professional Education Institute has been reviewed and approved as an Authorized Provider by the International Association for Continuing Education and Training (IACET). The Professional Education Institute has been awarded four of CEU's to participants who successfully complete this program.

VOLUME ONE
Laying The Foundation For Success

VOLUME TWO
Becoming A Real Estate Investor

DISCOVER

"To this day, I'm still excited every time I go out and look at a **new property**. *I know that, whether I'm purchasing residential or commercial properties, there are countless* **opportunities** *to increase my net worth and positive cash flow.*

For you, the **key** *is to start with properties you are familiar with. It's also important to* **find motivated sellers** *with whom you can attempt to negotiate* **win/win deals**. *Some of my most* **profitable transactions** *have been made with people who are relatively affluent, but are still very motivated to sell their property for reasons other than economic problems."*

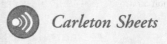 *Carleton Sheets*

FINDING PROPERTIES AND FLEXIBLE SELLERS

The attractiveness of property from an investment standpoint depends on the property itself, and on the willingness of the seller to be flexible when it comes to financing and/or price. Not all sellers are flexible, and finding them is a numbers game—you have keep at it to win.

There are many different types of properties that you can invest in, but certain types make better investments than others. When you search for a property that fits your investment profile, you should take into account the property's price, location, rent rate (for rental property), and features. When looking for properties, use the resources and information you currently have available.

When it comes to finding flexible sellers, you can either search for them or help them search for you. In both cases, your local newspaper and the Internet provide tremendous opportunities to do so. Business cards and flyers come in handy, too.

In this chapter, you will learn:

- How to locate potential investment properties.

- The importance of the property and the seller.

- Which types of properties are best for investment.

- What to look for in an investment property.

- How to locate flexible sellers and help them find you.

When you complete this chapter, you will be able to:

- Identify individuals and organizations that can provide marketplace information on two neighborhoods you have selected.

- Scout a neighborhood and ask specific questions to obtain information on its potential as an investment area.

- Identify the departments you should visit at your county courthouse and the information that each will provide.

- Take specific steps to advertise yourself as a real estate investor.

notes: _____

PROPERTIES, SELLERS, AND THE NUMBERS GAME

Finding properties that make good investments is a matter of locating the right property and seller and then playing a numbers game. To locate the right property and seller, you must seek out a *real property* that fits your *investment profile* that is currently owned by a seller who's willing to be flexible when it comes to financing and/or price. Playing the numbers game means being persistent—recognizing that most of the contacts you make will not result in locating a property you want to purchase—but they all will be educational.

The Importance of the Property and Seller

The attractiveness of any property from an investment standpoint is a function of two things—the property itself, and the situation of the seller who currently owns the property. If the property doesn't fit your investment profile or is located in a less desirable neighborhood, you need to find that out before you purchase it, not after. If the seller of the property is not flexible, you won't be able to buy the property creatively—that is, using my no money down techniques. Keep in mind though, that the seller's flexibility is constantly changing. A seller who is not flexible today may become flexible tomorrow.

Playing the Numbers Game

When you *farm* for properties you are playing a numbers game. By that I mean that out of all the sellers you contact, only a few are going to be flexible. It follows, then, that the more contacts you make, the better your chances of success. As a rule of thumb, you should set a goal of calling 25 sellers a week. Out of the 25 sellers, you might end up looking at only five properties, making an offer on three, and buying one.

The key to success in a numbers game is persistence. It can be discouraging, at times, to repeatedly come up short trying to find the right combination of property and seller. You must keep going—and always remind yourself that the next call could be the one!

> *"If you accumulate 30 homes over 10 years, sell half of them, and use the profits to pay down the mortgages on the others, your net worth could be close to $1 million with a positive cash flow of $10,000 a month."*

Remember—a few purchases a year, over time, can add up to big profits. If your goal is to buy several houses a year, you could potentially retire in 10 years just from purchasing homes in one or two large neighborhoods. For example, if you purchase three homes a year for 10 years, you will have 30 homes. If you then sell 15 of those 30 homes, you might use a portion of your profits to pay your tax obligation and to *pay down* the mortgages on the 15 remaining homes; perhaps even paying some of them off completely. You will then have 15 rental properties, either free and clear or with low mortgages. In 10 years, those 15 remaining

real property —Land, or building, and other improvements permanently attached to the land.

investment profile —The combined attributes of an investment property that you have identified as being right for you (e.g., single-family homes, three-bedrooms, within the northwest quadrant of the city).

farm —Cultivate a given geographic area by looking for property and flexible sellers.

pay down —To reduce the amount of principal on a loan.

notes:

houses will generate a significant monthly income, possibly $10,000 a month or more, and you should have a net worth approaching $1 million. I have had many students retire from their jobs and invest in real estate full time after investing for five years or less.

FINDING PROPERTIES

What makes a property attractive as an investment? That depends a lot on you and your goals. As a general rule, you should purchase only properties that you're comfortable owning. This rule applies not only to the type of property you buy, but to the size as well. If you feel comfortable owning single-family properties, you might want to stick with them until you feel confident to move on to something bigger. If you have experience purchasing small commercial properties, you might want to think twice before you purchase a 35-story bank building. On the other hand, if you have experience purchasing commercial property, then by all means continue to invest in that kind of property. You can find many up-to-date properties on my website—*www.CarletonSheets.com*.

Beyond your comfort level, you must make sure that you purchase only properties that will be profitable. If you don't do the proper analysis beforehand, you may end up with an *alligator*.

Types of Investment Property

Investment properties come in many shapes and sizes. Deciding which properties are best for your own situation and needs will help you focus your investing efforts on the most lucrative areas. In general, there are three types of property you can invest in—vacant land, commercial property, and residential property, including apartment buildings and single-family homes. As a beginning investor, you might want to pay special attention to *distressed properties*—for example, properties undergoing *foreclosure*. You may find that any one of the previously referenced types may be obtained through or outside of foreclosure.

Vacant Land

In some ways, owning vacant land seems to be part of the great American dream. Old sayings, like, "Buy land; they're not making any more of it," encourage people to go out and buy vacant land. And, if you know what you are doing, you can make money investing in vacant land. For example, you could buy a vacant tract of land and subdivide it into lots, double the price, and sell the lots for a large profit. You could even buy a vacant tract of land and develop it—that is, build on the land.

In general, though, vacant land is not a good investment. Even if you invest in a vacant plot of land and sell it in nine or 10 years for twice the purchase price,

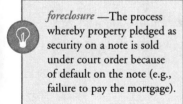

alligator —A property that has a substantial and continuing negative cash flow (i.e., it "eats" cash).

distressed property —A bargain property that is priced substantially below its present value or projected value when renovated.

foreclosure —The process whereby property pledged as security on a note is sold under court order because of default on the note (e.g., failure to pay the mortgage).

notes:

you haven't really made a lot of money. Why? Because vacant land produces no income to offset expenses. You also lose out on any potential interest you would have made by investing the money elsewhere. In addition, you must pay real estate taxes, selling expenses, maintenance costs, liability insurance, and special assessment costs. Sometimes, you even have to pay for special maintenance, such as removing vegetation from the property or cleaning up litter to conform to city and county codes. All in all, the average annual cost of owning a piece of vacant land could run as high as between 15% to 20% of what you paid for it.

Added to these direct costs is the indirect cost of inflation. The dollars you receive from the sale of the property are going to be worth less than the dollars you spent to acquire and maintain it. It turns out that if you can't sell the property for twice what you paid within two or three years, you are probably not going to make any money investing in vacant land.

Commercial Property

Commercial properties are those rented to tenants who conduct business. They are income properties for the owners because the tenants pay monthly or yearly rent. Some examples of commercial investment properties include:

- Hotels and motels
- Nursing homes
- Office buildings
- Post office buildings
- Restaurants
- Retail stores
- Shopping centers
- Warehouses

Some of these properties might seem obvious to you as income properties, while others will not. For example, most people are aware that investors own office buildings. Many are not aware, however, that many restaurants, stores, and even post office buildings are investor-owned. I even know of one religious congregation that leases its church from an investor. The lesson here is that, when it comes to income properties, the range of options is large.

Residential Property

Early in your real estate investing career, you will probably want to concentrate on residential properties—that is, properties in which people reside. For the beginning investor, single-family homes offer the best investment opportunity. When you have gained experience as an investor, you might want to try investing in larger multi-unit properties, like apartment buildings.

Single-Family Homes

Single-family homes are not only lower in cost, they are also plentiful in the marketplace. The best part is that many owners of single-family homes are flexible sellers.

notes:

cooperative — A form of ownership in which a corporation usually owns the building and land. The individual residents own the stock of the corporation and have a proprietary lease in a given unit or apartment.

Sales activity for all types of existing homes varies widely across the country, but there are more single-family homes sold than condominiums and *cooperatives* (also known as "co-ops"). In fact, nationwide, the demand for single-family homes represents a substantial portion of the total home market.

Apartment Buildings
Over the years, I've concentrated on investing in single-family homes and apartment buildings—I especially like apartment buildings because they allow me to gain maximum leverage with my time. That is, I can buy a 50-unit apartment building in about the same time frame that I can buy two or three single-family homes. It's also somewhat easier to deal with sellers of apartment buildings because they are generally more knowledgeable, and the opportunity for making large profits is much greater with apartment buildings than it is with single-family homes. Raising rents by just a few dollars on each apartment can increase the building's value by many thousands of dollars.

That's not to say that there aren't some disadvantages to owning apartment buildings—there are. The risks are greater, they are more management-intensive, and the mentality of the tenant is entirely different, which can result in much greater turnover. Maintenance costs can be higher, as some tenants are more likely to damage the property. In addition, finance terms may be less desirable. Despite all of these apparent shortcomings, once you have gained some experience investing, I encourage you to consider investing in apartment buildings or other multi-unit buildings.

"If you are a beginner, confine yourself to neighborhoods of single-family, two-unit or three-unit homes. If you are more seasoned, then add larger properties to your search."

Distressed Property
Distressed properties are those that, for one reason or another, are inexpensive due to the condition of the property or the situation of the seller. As you visit homes you're considering purchasing, you will find many homes that are inexpensive only because they are in need of cosmetic repairs. Some neighborhoods will also have multi-unit properties such as two-unit, three-unit, and four-unit rentals that fall into the same category.

Oftentimes, the owners of these properties are forced to sell because of high maintenance costs, mortgages with a high interest rate, job loss, divorce, death, or a host of other reasons. Because these homes exist in large numbers, finding flexible sellers in this market is not a difficult task.

notes:

What to Look for in a Property

You can't find something if you don't know what you're looking for. Basically, there are four things to look for in a potential investment property—price range, neighborhood, rent rates, and finally, the type of property and whether it fits a hole in the marketplace. Also, as you'll see a little later on, seller financing also plays a big part in the attractiveness of a property.

Price Range

Single-Family Homes

When it comes to price, single-family homes can be generally grouped into four broad categories: inexpensive, moderately expensive, expensive, and ultra-expensive. A good way to visualize their distribution in the market is to view the market as a pyramid, like that shown in Figure 7.1:

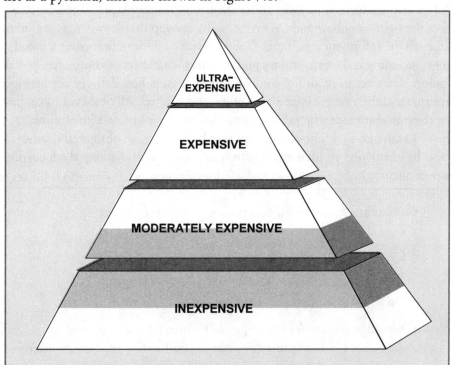

Figure 7.1: Market Distribution of Single-Family Homes

At the very top of the pyramid are the ultra-expensive properties, and at the bottom are all of the inexpensive properties. This graph illustrates the fact that there are far more inexpensive properties in the market than there are ultra-expensive ones. Consequently, common sense suggests that you are probably better off dealing with homes that are near the lower part of the pyramid, if only because there are more of them. In actual fact, your best bet is to concentrate on homes that fit in the region that falls between the upper part of the inexpensive category and the lower part of the moderately expensive category—that is, the shaded area in Figure 7.1. These types of properties are referred to as "bread-and-butter" properties because they are plentiful and in demand by the largest number of people.

notes:

Apartment Buildings

Apartment buildings make for good investments on a per-unit basis because their per-unit cost is lower than that of single-family homes. For example, an average home in your area might cost $150,000, while a two-unit rental property might cost $200,000, which works out to a per-unit cost of $100,000 ($200,000 divided by two). Generally, the lower the cost per unit, the easier you can structure a "no money down" purchase with a break-even or a positive cash flow.

Neighborhood

The choice of neighborhood can make or break a real estate investment. In general, you must make sure that you don't buy the right property in the wrong neighborhood or, for that matter, the wrong property in the right neighborhood.

Only when you have knowledge about the overall marketplace will you be able to select the right neighborhoods to invest in. To develop that knowledge, you must gather all the information you can. Good sources of information cover a broad range, including real estate brokers and investors, chambers of commerce, postal employees, tax assessors, utility company employees, police, delivery persons, local investment clubs, title insurance companies, and bankers. All of these sources have one thing in common: either directly or indirectly, their business involves real estate. To tap into their knowledge, you should approach all of them the same way—by identifying yourself as a relatively new investor and asking the following sorts of questions:

- "What are your general observations about the real estate market in this area?"

- "Do properties frequently appear on the market for sale and, if so, do they sell quickly?"

- "Do you live in this area? Do you like it?"

- "Would you consider investing in this area and, if you did, what kinds of properties would you buy?"

- "Are there areas where the real estate values seem to be going up faster than in others?"

- "Are there areas that you would stay away from as a real estate investor?"

In addition to gathering information from your sources, you should scout on your own for details. If you have lived in the same city for a number of years, you probably go to work the same way each day, shop at the same retail stores, and have a tendency to frequent the same areas. As a result, you probably know less about your city than you think you do. Here's some advice—learn to change your routine. You might be surprised at the opportunities you'll find just by

notes:

trying to become familiar with areas that are currently foreign to you. Make it a point to drive home a different way each day from work or shopping; if nothing else, you'll gain valuable information about the region you live in.

Rent Rates

For some reasons not fully understood, $100,000 homes in one area, for example, will rent for 10% to 20% less than $100,000 homes in another area. Since the marketplace dictates rent rates, it is difficult to purchase a home in one of these neighborhoods and offer it for rent at a rate 20% higher than other similar properties. It is important, therefore, to learn what rent rates are being paid in a given area.

Holes in the Marketplace

Any property that does not exist in great numbers, but is in great demand, is considered a hole in the marketplace. These are the properties that are the most easily rented and have the lowest vacancy rate; therefore, they make the best investments. Properties with fenced-in yards, garages, four or five bedrooms, fireplaces, central heat and air conditioning, and finished basements all fall into this category. For example, a four-bedroom home fills the needs of every prospective tenant who is looking for a two-bedroom home, but the reverse is not true. Therefore, a four-bedroom home is more easily rented than a two-bedroom home. Also, properties that are available for rent in the very best school districts or are located within a short commuting distance to popular places of employment are more easily rented. You might never find a property that possesses every one of these characteristics, but the more of these in-demand characteristics that a property has, the better investment it will be for you. As an aside, with the exception of two-bedroom condominiums and townhomes, I recommend that you not buy two-bedroom homes. They are not good investments because the number of potential tenants is limited and, while they can be easy to buy, they are usually difficult to sell. (Exceptions to this recommendation include neighborhoods surrounding colleges and universities, and known retirement communities.)

To a certain extent, you can create some of these characteristics after you buy the property. For example, you can fence in a yard or install central air conditioning in a home. However, it is certainly not practical to make a two-bedroom home into a five-bedroom home, and you cannot improve a school district or a commuting distance.

The factors that determine whether or not a property fills a hole in the marketplace often depend on the population distribution in an area. If you pay attention to population information, such as the average age of the people in a given area, you can buy and improve properties with distinctive features that attract the largest groups of potential renters. For example, consider the population information shown in Table 7.1:

notes:

Table 7.1: U.S. Population Distribution By Age Group (From U.S. Census Bureau)

Year	Total	Age 25–44	Age 45-64	Age 65 and Older
2000*	281,422,000	85,041,000 (30%)	61,952,000 (22%)	34,999,000 (12%)
2025*	337,815,000	86,106,000 (25%)	78,416,000 (23%)	62,641,000 (19%)
2050*	403,687,000	100,078,000 (25%)	89,089,000 (22%)	81,999,000 (20%)

*all figures rounded

The largest segment of the population for the country as a whole is between 25 and 44 years old. As time goes on, the number of people over the age of 45 will continue to increase, and the needs of the population, in general, will change accordingly. The first of the 76 million baby boomers in this country turned 50 in 1996, and the last of them will not turn 50 until 2014. Knowing the population distribution in your area, whether it's made up of growing families or people who are retired, will help you select properties that have the greatest chance of filling holes in the marketplace.

How to Find Potential Investment Properties

Finding investment properties is a matter of tapping your sources. I mentioned some of those sources before, like real estate brokers and investors. Others include newspapers, Internet listings, public records, personal and professional contacts, government agencies, and personal observation.

Newspapers

Most local newspapers carry a lot of real estate advertising and are very good sources for potential investment properties. In addition to advertising, newspapers also carry notices of public real estate auctions, many of which represent probate proceedings held to sell foreclosed or other types of distressed properties.

Other listings of interest to real estate investors include business news about executive promotions or transfers, plant expansions or downsizings, future planned developments, and miscellaneous listings such as weddings and birth announcements (in smaller places) are also a source of potential opportunity.

Internet Listings

The Internet is a great tool to use to locate properties. Many local real estate agencies have their own websites. You can use a search engine, such as Google (*www.google.com*) or the Yahoo! (*www.yahoo.com*) directory, to find the ones that pertain to your local area. These websites often include the area's current market offerings in detail. Many local newspaper websites also contain current area listings and some include archives where you can search for previous sales. Doing so can give you an idea of prices for specific neighborhoods and types of properties in your area.

notes:

Public Records

All real estate transactions should be legally recorded. You can look these up yourself at your county recorder's office. You might also find listings of publicly recorded real estate transactions on the Internet. For the quickest way to get information on properties from county, parish, or borough records across the country, visit *www.CarletonSheets.com*.

Personal and Professional Contacts

Other often overlooked sources for locating potential investment properties are your own family and friends. Don't be afraid to let them know that you are looking for properties. Also, don't forget your network of professional contacts—people you work with every day or people who belong to the same professional organizations that you do. There's nothing wrong with asking them for their help in locating properties. Talking to as many people as possible can expand your sources significantly.

Government Agencies

Government agencies can be a great help when it comes to finding properties. For example, you can contact the Department of Veteran Affairs (VA), the Federal Housing Administration (FHA), the Federal National Mortgage Association (Fannie Mae), or the Federal Home Loan Mortgage Corporation (Freddie Mac) for listings on their properties and foreclosures. Look particularly for properties that have favorable financing in addition to favorable locations. Included in this category would be any property that has existing assumable FHA or VA mortgages, conventional financing, owner financing, or no financing. All of these arrangements make the property easier to purchase.

It is now necessary to qualify for VA and FHA loans. One exception, according to VA Circular 26-90-37, is that you don't need VA approval if you buy on an *installment contract* or any other agreement in which title does not pass until the loan is paid. Always double-check with the appropriate government agency regarding the terms of the loan.

Personal Observation

Finally, don't forget that your car is one of your best tools for finding investment properties. To use it to its best advantage, obtain a map of your area from the local chamber of commerce, a bank, or a real estate broker, then go on your own personal scouting tour to learn more about your city and its neighborhoods. Your objective in doing so is to get acquainted with the layout of the areas where you will eventually make your investments. You do not have to drive long distances—in fact, you should try to confine your investing activities within a ten-mile radius of your home. If you are a beginner, confine yourself to neighborhoods of single-family, two-unit, or three-unit homes. If you are more seasoned, then add larger properties to your search.

installment contract—A way to sell a property in which the total sale price, or a specified portion of the sale price, is paid before a deed is transferred. (Also known as agreement for deed, contract for deed, or land contract.)

notes:

In addition to driving around and taking stock of the neighborhoods and homes, you should learn all you can from the people you meet who live and work there. Ask questions of people you see walking in the area—residents working in their yards, local retail storeowners and employees, or even a postal employee delivering mail in the neighborhood. You should adapt your questions to fit the circumstances of the person you are talking to, but in general, your questions should go something like this:

- "I'm thinking about buying property in this neighborhood. Tell me, do you live here? If so, have you lived here a long time?"

- "Do you rent or own?"

- "Are there many renters in this neighborhood?"

- "Do you have any idea of the price of homes in the area?"

- "Do you know what people are currently paying for rent in this neighborhood?"

- "What do you like most about the neighborhood? What do you like least?"

- "If you were to buy a rental property, would you buy it in this neighborhood? Why or why not?"

- "Do you know of any properties for sale or rent?"

You will be amazed at how much information you can develop about a neighborhood just by asking these questions. It's astounding what you can learn if you simply go out and talk to people!

FINDING FLEXIBLE SELLERS

To be successful as a real estate investor using the principles I teach in this course, you must be able to locate flexible sellers. In any given real estate market, approximately 80% to 85% of the sellers are firm on their asking prices and terms and are not willing to negotiate very much on either one. That means approximately 15% to 20% (and in some areas as much as 30%) of the sellers in the marketplace are flexible—many of them because they really do not want the properties they currently own.

Keep in mind that when you're looking for flexible sellers, a seller who is not flexible today might become so in the future—maybe even next week. Sellers are people, and just like everyone else, their emotions, needs, wants, desires, and situations are constantly changing. The more you meet and deal with potential sellers, the more attuned you'll become to how situations can change and how you can take advantage of the changes. For example, if a property owner is anxious to sell the property because of property management problems or because the owner does not want the property, you might be able to solve these problems and make the property profitable by smarter management. (For information about managing property the smart way, see Chapter 19, *Managing Property*.)

Types of Flexible Sellers

Flexible sellers are those who are willing to negotiate on price or terms, or sometimes even both. You will find it easiest to buy property by concentrating on these flexible sellers. Keep in mind that flexible sellers are not always "down and out." Sometimes even wealthy property owners can be flexible sellers, depending on their situations. Situations that produce flexible sellers include:

- Divorce
- Job transfer
- Estate sale
- Declining neighborhoods
- Unemployment
- Absentee ownership
- Property management problems
- Tenant problems
- Emotional dissatisfaction with the property

How to Find Flexible Sellers

Finding flexible sellers is not always easy. It takes persistence and creativity to find the flexible seller that matches your requirements. Sometimes, even sellers who are not flexible can be made flexible by offering a higher price for their properties in return for more favorable terms. If you can purchase their properties this way, you produce a win/win transaction that helps both sides.

When you put these techniques into practice, you are going to generate a lot of contact with sellers. Initially, 95% of your contact with sellers is going to be over the telephone. It is essential that you understand how to obtain as much information as possible over the telephone without offending the seller. You will save valuable time by doing so, and time is money. This is the focus of Chapter 8, *Gathering Information Over the Telephone*.

To find flexible sellers, you can look in the classified section of your local newspaper. Other resources include public records (at the county courthouse), banks, real estate agents, and your car. The Internet, too, can be an excellent resource for finding flexible sellers and for reviewing public records.

> *"Obstacles are those frightening things you see when you take your mind off your goals."*
>
> –Friedrich Wilhelm Nietzche

notes:

lease option —An agreement between two parties in which the party who owns the property sells to the second party the right to purchase the property at a future date. The second party lives in or subleases the property until the lease option expires.

Responding to Newspaper Ads Placed by Sellers

When you search the newspaper for real estate ads, pay close attention to how the ads are worded. Just the wording of their ads easily identifies many flexible sellers. For example, I once saw an ad that read, "Out of town seller must sell vacant house by 6 p.m. Sunday. I will be at property located at 103 Elm Street Saturday and Sunday between 9 a.m. and 6 p.m. Make offer." Another ad I once saw read, "Seller desperate. I will trade my property for anything that does not eat."

While these examples illustrate very blatant indications that the seller is flexible, most wording clues are more subtle. For example, any ad that you see that says "For sale or *lease option*," indicates a flexible seller because the ad actually tells you that if you do not want to purchase the property outright, the owner will consider a lease option. The wording also implies that the seller might be anxious to sell—which is to your advantage when negotiating terms. Other wording clues include the phrase, "will take property in trade" and/or multiple phone numbers in the ad, which might indicate that the seller has already occupied another property and needs to sell the advertised property as quickly as possible.

> *"Flexible sellers often advertise themselves. It's your job to recognize their flexibility."*

Finally, make sure to look for properties that have existing favorable financing which might allow you to purchase the property creatively with no money down. Also look for assumable mortgages or statements that the seller is willing to finance.

Just to give you a general idea of what ads placed by flexible sellers look like, I've put together a collection in Figure 7.2:

notes:

REAL ESTATE CLASSIFIEDS

EQUITY PARTICIPATION
Live in this home for $475 per month and qualify for 1/3 ownership.   555-5555

NO MONEY DOWN $40s
Anxious Owner will assist buyer with financing, 3 BRs., DR, eat-in kit, 100 ft lot, gas heat.   FRA Melmed Realtors   555-5555

PARK SLOPE by Owner, 2 fam, 3 flrs + bsmt, partly renov, lg yard. Owner will hold mtg. $128,000, $50,000 needed. 555-7000 ask for Mr. Jones

---

HELP ME I'M DOWN 2 bdrm home, N. Seattle
location, NOTHING DOWN. Take over payments, below market int., call now, Shorline inv., 24 hrs. 555-2023

PLANTATION
DESPERATE OWNER
3 bedrm, 2 bath ldg, eat-in kitchen. Fla rm, skylights, fishpond, lush landscaping, bring all offers.   555-6172

ASSUME LOW INTEREST
$79,950 Owner will assist in financing so you can take advantage of this LOW interest, fixed-rate mortgage. Private yard with fruit trees, garden strawberry patch, 2 baths, rec room, 2 frplcs, sun deck, and close to schools, shops, library. Vacant and ready for occupancy. Call for details on low down payment and interest!

F1615
DEL BIANCO REALTY, INC.
30821 Poc. Hwy. So.
555-1234   555-5555

2 FAMILY
Mortg assumption, So 13th St. alum sided. 5-6-1 cab kit, tiled bath, sep gas heat. $6,000 cash. Take over 7 1/2% FHA mortgage. 50 x 100 lot $27,000   555-5555

NOTHING DOWN
Marietta-Osborne High School district, 3BR, 1BA, C/A & A, 1/2 acre lot $667/month.   555-5555

Wissinoming   3   Bdrm,   2   Bth   Single
HANDYMAN SPECIAL
Asking $25,000   Open   to   Offer
Century   21   Beacon   Realty   555-1600

RUMSON--Unusual Tudor-style home on dbl lot, 100' x 168'. Minstrel gallery overlks cath ceil main rm w/WBFP. 4BR, 2 bth, rec rm, laun, wrkshp. Sep tool shed & dbl gar. 2nd lot may be blt upon. $160,000. 555-1168

WAYNE-Rent opt to buy 1BR condo, laun rm, fpl
555-0394   leave message

ACADEMY Rd Vic   9% Mortgage Latham Park, 3 bdrms, sunken livrm, ultra kitchen, fin bsmt, w/w cpts. Only $44,900 Assume Mtg.
AMERICA Corp., Rltrs   555-5555

ANDREWS GARDENS--N. 413 NW 46th Ct, 2 bedrm 2 bath, immaculate, will finance, $62,500. 555-5555

Investor Liquidation
Owner retiring to Florida. Several desirable Properties Available. Call Eugene. 555-5555

Figure 7.2: Real Estate Classified Ads
Can you spot the words that indicate the ad was placed by a flexible seller?

Searching Public Records
Your county courthouse is a veritable gold mine of information for you, the real estate investor, particularly in smaller towns. When you visit your courthouse (and you should do so soon), you should concentrate on three or four departments—the recorder's office, the county tax collector's office, the clerk of the court, and the real estate assessor's office.

- The recorder's office—can give you the names of the past and present owners, how much was paid each time the property was sold, and the financial aspects of each transaction. They will also have information regarding any liens or judgments against the properties.
  Note: you may want to bring an address with you to look up while you are there.

- The county collector's office—usually handles *tax liens* against properties with unpaid taxes.

tax lien —A lien imposed against real property for the non-payment of taxes, both real estate and income taxes.

notes:

- The clerk of the court's office—can furnish information on any mortgage foreclosure, including remaining balance, the original balance, the lender and lender's attorney, plus the name and address of the defaulting parties. You can go to *www.CarletonSheets.com* to find foreclosure properties.

- The assessor's office—has the most complete information on properties. They can give you the assessed value of a property, the square footage, any improvements, and the lot size. They can even give you the name of the person paying the taxes, which is usually the owner, and much, much more. Many assessors maintain an assessment card (a record that has a diagram of the property, including all improvements). Some of the information usually found in the tax assessor's files, which is public information, accessible by anyone, is:

  - Ownership history and current taxpayer.
  - Details of construction.
  - Date original occupancy permit issued.
  - Plot plan showing location and size of improvements.
  - Value breakdown between land improvements.
  - Assessment and history of assessment.
  - Number and dimensions of rooms.
  - When sold and sale price.
  - Parcel identification number (PIN), also referred to as Land Serial Number (LSN) in some areas of the country, or Assessors Parcel Number (APN).

Seeing Banks as Flexible Sellers

Banks, too, can be flexible sellers. They own property as a result of foreclosures. If they think you can solve their problem by purchasing these properties, banks can be very cooperative when working with you.

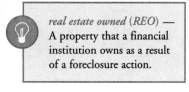

real estate owned (REO) — A property that a financial institution owns as a result of a foreclosure action.

Properties owned by banks are known as *real estate owned* (REO) properties. When you talk to a banker about REO properties, the banker is likely to tell you that the bank wants a fixed price for the property and wants it all in cash. Don't take the news at face value, though. Bankers are usually willing to negotiate not only on the total selling price, but on the terms as well. Often, banks will loan money to you to buy the property and, in some cases, to fix it up. By the way, I have even known bankers that have been willing to lease option REO properties.

Working With Real Estate Brokers or Agents

Some people refuse to work with real estate brokers or agents because they think it will add unnecessary costs to acquiring the property. Many times, though, for every dollar they try to save in a real estate brokerage commission, they end up losing several dollars in real estate profits. I have no qualms about working with

notes:

brokers or agents. They can be your ears, eyes, and legs in finding investment opportunities. Remember, brokers or agents often have timely and computerized information available to them that you do not. Therefore, the advantage of working with them is that they save you time, have resources to find the best properties for your needs, and help you along the way to your purchase.

Many real estate brokers belong to the National Association of Realtors and are known as Realtors. They also belong to the state and local boards of Realtors and to the Multiple Listing Service (MLS). These association and board memberships provide Realtors with up-to-date information about the industry to better help their clients.

When a local broker belongs to the MLS, he or she agrees to share listings with all other local broker members. Property listings taken by these Realtors must be processed into the bimonthly (or weekly, in some areas of the country) MLS listing book or website, which are good sources for finding properties. Keep in mind that some of the listings are already sold by the time the MLS book is printed and distributed, or is available on the web. However, because most brokers' offices are computerized, you can get the most current information at the broker's office right from the computer even before listings are published in the MLS book. In fact, Internet websites listing properties for sale are proliferating at an outstanding rate and could eventually replace the local MLS system.

Driving Through Neighborhoods

As I discussed earlier in this chapter, your car can be a tremendous tool when searching for investment opportunities. When you're scouting neighborhoods, make it a practice of looking for properties and flexible sellers. Drive through the neighborhoods often, and become familiar with their boundaries, schools, bus stops, employment centers, shopping areas, access to expressways, and recreational areas. If you drive through a particular neighborhood once or twice a week, you will see a lot of real estate related activity. Take note of people moving in and out of the area, new "For Sale" and "For Lease" signs, and properties that have sold. Also, whenever possible, stop and get acquainted with people walking in the neighborhood or working in their yards. Ask the questions I recommended earlier in this chapter. Leave a business card with them and ask them to call you if they hear of anything that is for sale. You might even offer to pay them $100 for a lead on any property that you ultimately purchase.

Helping Sellers Find You

Instead of actively searching for sellers, it's sometimes better to help the sellers find you. Again, your local newspaper can come to your aid in this regard. You can place an ad in the classified section stating that you are interested in finding a property with flexible financing. Something as simple as properly phrased business cards can open many doors, too. You might also consider creating a flyer.

notes:

Finally, you might want to consider developing an Internet home page that highlights your interests as an investor who is always looking for properties with flexible sellers. If you do, you should add some references or samples of previous properties you have purchased.

Placing Newspaper Ads to Buy Property

Many of my students attest to the fact that placing ads in newspapers is a very effective method of attracting sellers. Rather than spending time going through the real estate classified ad section looking for flexible sellers, you can place your own ad in the newspaper and attract them to you. This method of informing the public that you are a real estate investor can be an effective and low-cost way to solicit responses.

When writing your ad, be careful not to appear too slick. Such ads can have a negative effect on the reader because they appear to be from someone who might take advantage of anyone who responds.

When someone responds to your ad, you will probably be asked what you mean by flexible financing. Don't ever attempt to explain what this means over the telephone. Just say that it depends on the situation and move directly on to pre-qualifying the seller and the property over the phone using the techniques I describe in Chapter 8, *Gathering Information Over the Telephone*.

Newspaper ads can also come in handy when you're selling property. For example, you could run an ad that is very open-ended to attract as many potential buyers as possible.

Placing Newspaper Ads to Sell Property

Since you cannot stay by your telephone every minute to take the calls that come in, your best bet is to invest in an inexpensive telephone answering machine. Your recorded message could say, "Hello, this is [your name]. I'm sorry I'm not here to take your call right now, but if you leave your name and telephone number, I'll get back to you as soon as I return." If you have a separate phone line to use for your investing and selling, you can further customize your message to encourage people to leave their names and numbers—for example, "I have several attractive homes that are very affordable in both price and terms."

When you talk to anyone who responds to your ad, attempt to learn as much about the caller as you can. This information will help you match the property you have for sale to the needs of the caller and, if no match can be made, to consider the caller as a potential buyer for a property you might acquire in the future. Here are a few questions you can ask (make sure you are polite):

- "What kind of property are you looking for?" (Explain that you're a private investor and own many different properties. Try to determine what the caller's space requirements are and any particular features for which he or she is searching.)

notes:

- "What area would you like to live in?"

- "What's your general price range?"

- "In order to match your needs to the existing financing on my properties, I'd like to ask what the largest monthly payment your budget will allow is?"

- "Can you afford to make a down payment? If so, how much can you afford?"

- "Where do you work? How long have you been employed there?" (Explain that you need to get some background information to determine if and how much financing you can afford to offer.)

- "Have you ever owned a home before? If so, how long did you own your home? Have you ever leased a property with a purchase option?"

- "Have you ever been through a foreclosure or a bankruptcy before?"

To repeat, make sure to be polite and ask the questions in a conversational manner. If it sounds like you're reading them from a list, the telephone interview may seem awkward and artificial, and you'll have a hard time getting the information you need.

Even if the caller indicates that he or she is not interested in the property you have available at the moment, continue the interview anyway. You might still be able to help them locate a property that fits his or her needs. When you find such a property, you could negotiate to purchase it with a contract *contingency* that states, "Subject to a final inspection by the purchaser and written acceptance of same within 72 hours of the seller's acceptance of this contract." That should give you ample time to show the house to your prospective purchaser. (See Chapter 13, *Making the Offer and Negotiating,* for information on contract contingencies.)

contingency—A provision within a contract that makes performance under the contract conditioned upon the occurrence or non-occurrence of a stated event.

Passing Out Business Cards
Most people who are self-employed or who work for a company have a business card. Business cards are great because they tell the world about the nature of your business or profession. They're also inexpensive. You can have a card printed that says, "I buy real estate," or "I am a real estate investor," or "I buy and sell houses." Business cards help create a professional image. In addition to announcing that you buy real estate, your card might include, "I also have houses for sale and lease. I am not a real estate broker." Also, consider adding, "I am a private investor." If you do not add this fact, people might not contact you because they might assume that you are a broker or agent and they would have to pay a commission for buying or leasing property through you.

notes:

Don't be bashful about using your cards. Your success as a real estate investor largely depends upon how well you succeed in letting the world know you are in business. Pass them out to all the merchants with whom you do business—for example, your service station attendant, druggist, grocery store employees, hairdresser or barber, dry cleaner, and your mail carrier. In fact, you should make a list of all the business and service people you come in contact with on a daily or weekly basis and make a point of getting your business card to everyone on the list. You might be surprised at how many people that is.

Make a habit of handing your card out at garage sales (frequently, they are held by people who are thinking about moving), and to insurance company representatives, your local clergy, and personnel offices at local industries. Take advantage of any situation—such as giving them to people you may be standing in line with at your local supermarket or pharmacy. After giving someone you meet a card that says, "I buy real estate," you can ask them, "Do you have any property for sale or do you know anyone who does?" Even if people do not have property to sell at the moment, they will remember you and possibly contact you later when they do have some real estate to sell.

> *"This is not a 'needle in a haystack' exercise. Two out of every three people you talk to are either going to buy, sell, or lease real estate or know someone who is."*

Another way to distribute your business cards is to place them on bulletin boards in supermarkets or discount stores. These high volume stores have an enormous amount of traffic. Anything placed on the stores' bulletin boards will receive a lot of exposure.

Distributing Flyers

Flyers can be used very much like business cards. They're better, though, for blanketing an area because they allow you the opportunity to include more information and an eye-catching design. A sketch of a home or a clever design on a full-size sheet of paper can be a dramatic way to introduce yourself as an investor. An art student at a local high school or college could help you design a flyer that is uniquely yours.

You can pass out flyers door-to-door or place a stack of flyers in local retail stores so that customers can help themselves. Check local ordinances before you do this, though, because some communities require a permit to do so. One of my students once had a flyer printed on heavy paper stock, cut a hole in the top, and made doorknob hangers.

notes:

Finally, keep in mind that using flyers puts you back in the numbers game. If you pass out 1,000 flyers, you may get 15 or 20 calls, look at three or four specific properties, and buy one.

REVIEW
Summary

When evaluating whether or not a property is an attractive investment, you should take into consideration two things—the property itself, and the willingness of the seller to be flexible when it comes to financing and/or price. Not all sellers are flexible, and finding them is a numbers game. If you call 25, you might make offers on five properties and end up buying only one. That's why you have to make as many contacts as you can.

There are many different types of properties that you can invest in, including vacant land, income property, single-family homes, and distressed property. Vacant land is not a good investment, in general, but the other types can be if you know what to look for before you buy.

When you search for an investment property, you should take into account its price, neighborhood, rent rate, and its type and size. Your best bet is to focus on properties that are somewhere between inexpensive and moderately expensive because they make up a big part of the market and can produce handsome profits. You should never buy what seems like the right home in the wrong neighborhood or the wrong home in the right neighborhood. If you're purchasing income property, you need to make sure that the rent rates in the area where the property is located will ensure a profitable investment. Finally, you should look for properties that fill holes in the marketplace—that is, homes that don't exist in great numbers, but for which the demand is high.

To find properties, you should make use of the many sources of information that are available to you, like newspapers and the Internet, as well as your car. When it comes to finding flexible sellers, you can either search for them or help them search for you. In both cases, your local newspaper and the Internet provide tremendous opportunities to do so. Business cards and flyers come in handy, too.

Questions

- Why is vacant land usually not a good investment? (See page 7-2.)

- Why are single-family homes the best properties for new investors? (See page 7-3.)

- What are two of the advantages and two of the disadvantages of investing in an apartment building? (See page 7-4.)

notes:

- Who should you contact to increase your knowledge of a specific marketplace? (See page 7-6.)

- What is a hole in the marketplace and why is it important to you as an investor? (See page 7-7.)

- What are three of the ways to find potential properties? (See page 7-8.)

- What are three of the questions you should ask when scouting a neighborhood for potential properties? (See page 7-10.)

- What is a flexible seller and what are three situations that would make a seller flexible? (See page 7-10.)

- What are five resources at your disposal for finding flexible sellers? (See page 7-11.)

ACTION STEPS

1. Compile a list of individuals and organizations that can provide marketplace information about two different neighborhoods.

2. Contact the people on the list and use the questions in this chapter to gather information on the two neighborhoods.

3. Scout the two neighborhoods using the questions in this chapter to obtain information on their potential as investment areas.

4. Take an afternoon and visit your county courthouse and acquaint yourself with its layout, the information it contains, and the people who work in the tax assessor's office, the recorder's office, and the department that handles foreclosures.

5. Have a set of flyers printed and distribute them at local stores.

6. Place an ad in your local newspaper advertising yourself as an investor interested in finding properties to buy.

7. Go to *www.CarletonSheets.com* to get up-to-date information quickly.

notes:

FINAL COMMENTS

The more you know about the marketplace, the more likely you are to find properties that offer investment potential. You have a limited amount of time to spend looking for a house or investment property, so it is important to spend that time wisely and productively. Remember, only 15% to 20% of the sellers you contact will be flexible. To spend time with sellers that are inflexible could be an exercise in futility. But remember, though, that sellers' needs and wants could change on a daily or weekly basis. So a seller who is not flexible today, could become that way tomorrow.

NOTES

INTERVIEW

*"It's so **important** to find out if the property you found in the newspaper or online could be a **potentially profitable** investment.*

*When I call to inquire about a property for sale, I know within a **matter of minutes** whether or not it's one I want to pursue.*

*By asking the **right questions** about the property over the **phone**, you can save yourself a wasted trip. There is nothing more **valuable** to you as an investor than your **time**. Many of my students have used my telephone techniques to better utilize their time and **accomplish** more in the time they have available for real estate investing."*

 *Carleton Sheets*

GATHERING INFORMATION OVER THE TELEPHONE

Your telephone is one of the most powerful tools you have as a real estate investor. By making calls to prospective sellers and obtaining the right kinds of information, you can avoid pursuing bad investments. To obtain the right information, however, you must ask the right questions—and you must know how to politely direct a conversation over the telephone. You must also record and keep track of the information you obtain. The *Seller Information Form* included in my *Real Estate Forms Portfolio* provides a handy means of doing both.

In this chapter, you will learn:

- The importance of gathering information about prospective properties.

- The four key types of information you need to learn.

- How to record and organize the information you obtain.

- The importance of good telephone etiquette.

- How to respond to an answering machine.

- What kind of greeting to leave on your answering machine.

- How to use the *Seller Information Form* in my *Real Estate Forms Portfolio* to guide you through the process of gathering information over the telephone.

When you complete this chapter, you will be able to:

- Conduct telephone interviews with sellers to prequalify them.

- Use the telephone to gain valuable information and save time.

I have included in this chapter three actual (edited) telephone conversations that I have had with prospective sellers. These conversations serve as examples of the principles I describe.

THE IMPORTANCE OF GATHERING INFORMATION

Knowledge and information are vital to any successful endeavor. To succeed as a real estate investor, you must know how to obtain information on properties and sellers quickly and efficiently, and how to evaluate the information you obtain.

Before you go to the trouble to visit a prospective property, you should always contact the seller by phone and gather information about the property, the financing, and the seller's own situation. If a broker or agent is involved, you should also find out as much as you can about their willingness to participate in financing your purchase of the property.

In addition to asking questions over the telephone, you must also learn how to record and organize the information you receive.

Recording the Information

If you don't have a photographic memory, the information you gather over the telephone will be useless to you unless you record it in some kind of organized fashion. To help you keep track of the information you gather, my *Real Estate Forms Portfolio* includes a *Seller Information Form* (Figure 8.1), where you can write down the seller's answers to the questions you ask. The form also serves as a roadmap to guide you through the conversation and make sure you get all the information you need. (For a description of the form, see the section with the heading: *Using the Seller Information Form.*)

Organizing the Information

Unless you make only one telephone contact to a seller in your lifetime, you'll need a system of organizing the *Seller Information Forms* after you fill them out. If you have only a few forms to organize, paper clips and sticky notes will do. As your investment career grows, however, and the forms pile up, you should consider filing them in file folders.

No matter how you store the forms, you should group them according to seller classification:

- Good
- Flexible
- Inflexible
- Rejected

"Good" forms identify sellers who are flexible on both price and financing, and whose properties seem worth visiting based on the information you gathered over the telephone. "Flexible" forms are those for which the seller is flexible but the property might be of questionable value. "Inflexible" forms identify situations where the property might be of interest but the seller is inflexible at the moment. (Keep in mind that a seller who is currently inflexible might become flexible in the near future as his or her situation changes.) "Rejected" forms identify sellers who are inflexible and whose properties are of questionable value—in short, sellers you don't want to contact again. Why even keep a record of this last group? Because the seller of the property might change the ad, and you may not recognize it as being one you have already contacted. The property's address is probably the best clue in recognizing this as a property that you made calls about earlier.

TELEPHONE ETIQUETTE

When gathering information over the telephone, you should always follow two simple rules:

- Be polite
- Be a good listener

These rules not only help you establish a rapport with the person on the other end of the telephone line, they greatly enhance your efficiency in obtaining the information you need.

Being Polite
People are generally more willing to share information with those who show them respect than with those who are rude. Rudeness of any sort throws up barriers between people in any conversation, and those barriers can make even the most straightforward information difficult to obtain. So—be polite and respectful.

Being a Good Listener
One of the best ways to develop a rapport with anyone is to be an empathetic listener. In general, sellers will share information more easily with callers who demonstrate sensitivity than they will with callers who are strictly businesslike. As the conversation progresses, and you learn about the property and seller, try to imagine yourself in his or her situation and to understand what it feels like to be in his or her shoes. By demonstrating this kind of sensitivity, you can quickly open up the channels of communication. Always listen empathetically and respond compassionately.

Responding to an Answering Machine
When you reach a seller's answering machine, leave a message saying you are interested in a property, along with your first name and phone number—repeating it twice (say it slowly and clearly). Also, ask the seller to get back to you as soon as possible.

notes:

WHAT YOU NEED TO FIND OUT
Four Key Types of Information

To determine whether or not a lead is worth pursuing, you need to evaluate its potential as an investment. To do so, you must obtain four key types of information about the lead:

- Property
- Financing
- Seller
- Broker or agent (if one is involved in the transaction)

Property information includes the basic description of the property itself, the characteristics of the neighborhood, the current rental situation, if any, and how long the property has been on the market. Financing information describes the current financing of the property and the willingness of the seller to participate in financing your purchase. Seller information provides background data on the seller's situation, especially with regard to his or her reason for selling. Broker or agent information includes the willingness of the broker or agent to participate in the financing by taking his or her commission as a *note* and/or loaning you money for the down payment.

note —The legal evidence of debt.

> *"Determining a seller's wants and needs are the result of listening carefully rather than making assumptions."*

Using the Seller Information Form

The *Seller Information Form* found in my *Real Estate Forms Portfolio* is designed to help you gather, record, and catalogue information obtained over the phone from prospective sellers. It includes 13 general items that cover all four key types of information listed previously. To help you get the most from the form, I've put together a list of recommended questions, as well as some tips on how to handle the conversation.

SELLER INFORMATION FORM

Seller: ☑ Good ☐ Flexible
☐ Rejected ☐ Inflexible

Source or Lead ___Newspaper (Globe)___

Property Address ___123 Main Street___ Date ___March 3___

___Anywhere, USA___ Phone ___555-5555___

1. Seller's Name ___Joe and Mary Seller___

2. Property

    A. Size (Sq. ft.) ___1400___

    B. Total Rooms ___7___

    C. Layout ___Ranch___ Bedrooms ___3___ Baths: Full ___1___ Half ___1___

    D. Lot Size ___60x120___

    E. Garage ___Detached___ Size ___20x20___

    F. Special Features ___nice landscaping-well maintained___

    G. Appliances Included, etc. ___built in refrigerator stove and oven___

3. Price $ ___150,000___

4. Existing Financing

    A. Assumable ___maybe (VA Loan)___

    B. Lender ___First Federal S&L___ Original Loan Balance $ ___$70,000___

    C. Payment Current ___$513.00___ Current Loan Balance $ ___About $50,000___

5. Will Seller Assist Financing ___some___ Cash Needed ___$50-65,000___

6. How Long on Market ___5 months___

7. How Long Owned ___16 years___

8. Why Selling ___retirement-relocation___

9. Like Most ___great neighborhood___ Like Least ___yard work___

10. Renters in Neighborhood ___some___ Neighborhood Rent Rates ___unknown___

11. Estimated Rental Value ___$1500 monthly___

    Lease/Option ___consider___

12. Cash Deal, Quick Close Price $ ___$140,000___

13. Broker Involved:

    Name ___Henry Broker___ Phone ___555-6666___

    Background ___extensive___

    Could Manage ___yes___

    Management Fee ___10%___ Vacancy Rate ___minimal___

    Any Other Investment Properties ___yes, several___

    Will Take Commission Over Time ___no___

Figure 8.1: Example *Seller Information Form*

notes:

Recommended Questions

The following table lists each of the items on the *Seller Information Form* along with recommended questions for obtaining the related information:

Table 8.1: Recommended Questions

Item	Recommended Question(s)
1. Seller's name	• Hi, my name is [your name]. May I ask your name?
2. Property	• Can you tell me about your home (or property)? • What is the size and square footage of the house? • What is the layout of the house (for example, split plan, ranch, or two-story)? • What is the lot size? • Does it have a garage? • How many rooms are there in the home? • How many bedrooms and bathrooms does it have? • Are there features of the home that are special or set it apart? • What appliances or pieces of furniture are included with the property?
3. Price	• How much are you asking for the property? • May I ask how you arrived at that price?
4. Existing financing	• What existing financing is on the property? • Is the loan assumable? • Who is the lender? • What are the terms, interest rate, and monthly payments? • If you don't mind my asking, are you current on all of your payments?
5. Seller assisted financing	• Are you willing to assist in the financing? • Do you need cash at the time of closing? If so, how much do you need (and may I ask the nature of the need)? • Would it be possible to spread the down payment over a period of time?
6. Time on market	• How long has the property been on the market?

" The key to wisdom is knowing the right questions. "

-John A. Simone, Jr.

notes:

7. Length of ownership	•Have you owned the property for a long time?
8. Reason for sale	•Sounds like a nice property. May I ask, why are you selling?
9. Property preferences	•What do you like most about your property? •What do you like least?
10. Renters in neighborhood	•Are there any renters in your neighborhood? If so, do you happen to know what they are paying in rent? •What do you think the rent would be for your property?
11. Lease option	•Would you consider leasing your property with an option to buy?
12. Cash deal	•If I were able to buy your property for all cash and close on it within a week, what is the very lowest price you would consider taking? (This question suggests to the seller that you could pay cash for the property, even if you cannot. Use this question cautiously if you are not paying cash and you absolutely need seller financing.)
13. If a broker or agent is involved *(questions for the broker or agent)*	•Do you own any investment property yourself? •Have you ever owned any investment property? •Does your firm manage properties? •If I bought this property, would you consider managing it for me? If so, what would you charge to do so? •What is the vacancy rate in the area? •If rented—based on your managing experience, would the rent currently being charged for this property be above market, below market, or just right? •Do you have any other properties for sale that might be good investments for me—for example, some that are physically distressed or owned by someone who is very anxious to sell? •Would you be willing to take all or part of your commission in the form of a note? (If you [the caller] are a licensed broker or agent, ask if he or she would be willing to split their share of the commission with you.)

The first few questions on the *Seller Information Form* establish a rapport with the seller because they're easy to answer, and the answers concern things that the seller should already know or be able to find out. Other questions, such as whether or not the seller is willing to participate in financing your purchase, require more thinking on the part of the seller—especially if he or she is unfamiliar with the options available to do so. That's why a seller shouldn't be asked until the rapport is already established.

Conversational Tips
Always phrase the questions in a positive, conversational tone and, where natural, precede with the seller's first name. For example, instead of saying, "I don't suppose you know whether anyone in your neighborhood is renting," simply ask, "Elizabeth, do you know if there are any renters in the neighborhood?"

As soon as you end a call, summarize your notes and make a note on the form classifying the property as good or rejected, and the seller as flexible or inflexible. Regardless of the seller's classification, forms that describe good properties should be retained in your "hold" file, and forms that describe rejected properties should be filed separately.

If the answers you receive in your telephone call prompt you to set up a visit to the property, transfer the information from the *Seller Information Form* to a *Property Analysis Form* (Figure 8.2), and take it with you when you visit. The *Property Analysis Form* includes five sections that cover everything from the owner's name and address to specific information on the property's current financing. When you complete all sections of the *Property Analysis Form*, you will have an excellent perspective on all aspects of the property.

PROPERTY ANALYSIS FORM

1. OWNERSHIP AND PROPERTY LOCATION

Owner's Name ___Saundra Seller___ Telephone ___123-4567___

Owner's Address ___1737 Main Street, Anywhere, USA___

Property Address ___same as above___

2. PHYSICAL DESCRIPTION

Size in Square Feet ___1,400___ Bedrooms ___3___ Bath: Full ___1___ Half ___1___

Appliances   Refrigerator ___yes___   Stove ___yes___   Oven ___yes___

                  Washer/Dryer ___yes___   Water Softener _____

                  Microwave _____   Garbage Disposal ___yes___

                  Dishwasher ___yes___   Other ___none___

Basement ___No___   Attic ___partial___   Porch ___yes___   Utility Room ___yes___

Garage ___2 car attached___   Den/Family Room ___yes___   Lot Size ___50x150___   Zoning ___S.F. Residential___

Fireplace ___1___   Window Coverings ___none___

Carpet ___Fair condition___   Construction ___Brick/cedarsiding___   Age ___15 years___

Central AC ___yes___   Heat ___yes___   Largest Utility Bill ___$135/month___

City Water ___yes___   School District ___Wheatland___

Public Transportation ___Bus 1 block___   Taxes ___$1850.___   Year ___2002___

Assessments _____   Items Included in Assessment _____

Comments ___well maintained-great curb appeal___

3. OWNER'S SITUATION

How Long Owned ___15 years___   How Long on Market ___35 days___   Asking Price $___150,000___

Original Asking Price $___150,000___   Date of Price Change _____

Why Selling ___job transfer___   Needs Cash ___yes___

How Much Cash ___entire equity___   Could Cash be Spread Over Time ___maybe___

What Owner Will be Doing With Cash Received ___new home in new city___

Will Owner Assist In Financing ___a little maybe___   How Much ___$10,000___

Interest Rate ___10%___

What Owner Likes Most About Property ___lot___   Least ___cutting grass___

Comments ___great neighborhood___

4. RENTAL ANALYSIS

Is Property Rented Now ___no___   To Whom _____   Children _____   Pets _____

How Long _____   Lease or Month to Month _____

Monthly Rent _____   Last Increase _____   Last Month's Rent _____

Security Deposit _____   Concessions _____

Potential Rental Income ___$1,500/month___   Improvements Needed Before Renting ___none known___

Other Rents in Neighborhood ___$1,200-1,600/month___   Rent Paid _____

Comments ___will make excellent rental property___

5. FINANCING

First Mortgage ___yes___   Lender ___First United___   Balance ___$42,000___

    Interest Rate ___11%___   Assumable _____   Payment ___$399.98___

    P.I.T.I.* ___$180/month___   Debt Service Constant ___10.98%___

Second Mortgage ___none___   Lender _____   Balance _____

    Interest Rate _____   Assumable _____   Payment _____

    Debt Service Constant _____

Other Liens ___ABC Construction $2,500 mechanics lien to be paid at closing___

*Principal, Interest, Taxes, and Insurance

Figure 8.2: Example *Property Analysis Form*

notes:

EXAMPLE CONVERSATIONS

The methods for gathering information over the telephone are best illustrated by examples of actual telephone conversations. This section includes three such actual (edited) conversations between prospective sellers and me. The three sellers included here are:

- Helen—Real estate broker
- Eileen—Seller facing foreclosure
- Dick—Owner of a home with rental units

Each telephone conversation represents a unique situation with regard to the property and/or seller. In each case, I demonstrate how to politely and directly steer the conversation toward obtaining the information needed to determine the flexibility of the seller and the attractiveness of the property from an investment standpoint.

Helen—Real Estate Broker
Background
Helen is a real estate broker who represents the owner of a single-family income property. The newspaper ad that prompted my call reads as follows:

> DOWNTOWN. 3 BEDROOM/ 1 BATH. SCREENED
> PATIO. TENANT OCCUPIED. SELLER WILL HOLD
> MORTGAGE WITH $5,000 DOWN.
> ASKING $39,000. BAKER REALTY, 555-4567

Telephone Conversation

Helen: Baker Realty. May I help you?

Carleton: Yes, ma'am. I'm calling about the three-bedroom, one-bath with screened patio that you have advertised in Boynton Beach. Is there anyone there who can help me with that? It's listed as $5,000 down, $39,000 asking price.

Helen: I can help you with that.

Carleton: By the way, my name is Carleton. May I ask your first name?

Helen: My name is Helen.

Carleton: Can you describe the property to me, Helen? Are there any special features that make it stand out?

notes:

Helen: It's three bedrooms and one bath, and basically the house is a CBS (concrete block/stucco) house—an older home. Apparently, there was some fire damage sometime back, and when they did the repairs, they added aluminum siding on the side of the house where the other bedroom is. So originally, the house was a two-bedroom, one-bath, and then they added another bedroom.

Carleton: Does it look like a temporary structure in any way?

Helen: Oh, no. It's all secured. And behind that is also a dining area and a screened-in patio.

Carleton: Oh, I see.

Helen: The kitchen and the living room and the two bedrooms and one bath are in the main part of the house—the original construction.

Carleton: And what appliances are included with the property?

Helen: There's a range and refrigerator, along with an air conditioning unit.

Carleton: Is there a garage or carport?

Helen: No, there isn't.

Carleton: What about the existing financing?

Helen: There's no financing on it at this time. The owner is willing to take cash for it. He's also willing to hold paper on it. He told us when we took the listing that he will hold paper with a $5,000 down payment and a mortgage of approximately 12%, but I think he would take less than that for another mortgage.

Carleton: So you think he's willing to take a $34,000 mortgage?

Helen: Right.

Carleton: Helen, I'm a real estate investor, and I'm always looking for properties that I think will make good investment properties as rentals.

Helen: Okay.

Carleton: Do you think the seller might be willing to assist even more in the financing than the $34,000?

Helen: He might, yes.

notes:

Carleton: He's a pretty flexible seller, then.

Helen: He sounds like he is. He's living up in Georgia, and he's got this property down here and, basically, he wants to get out of managing here in the area.

Carleton: What is the property currently rented for?

Helen: Presently, it's rented for $450 a month.

Carleton: And how long have the tenants been there?

Helen: They've been there for quite a while, it seems. He tells us over six years.

Carleton: That sounds like a pretty good opportunity.

Helen: Yes, it does.

Carleton: How long has the property been on the market?

Helen: About a month—month and a half.

Carleton: Has he owned the property long, do you know?

Helen: From what I understand, yes. As to how long, I can't say. He has told us that this is the last property that he has here in Boynton Beach, and he wants to liquidate. He wants to get everything up into the Georgia area, where he lives now.

Carleton: So he's selling because he's an absentee owner.

Helen: Right.

Carleton: Are there any other renters in that neighborhood?

Helen: I don't know, offhand. We did meet the lady across the street, and she's been there for a long while. It's an older area of Boynton. I'll give you the address and then you can, you know, at least go by it.

Carleton: Before you do, let me ask you this. Do you think the present owner would consider a lease option on the property at all? In other words, lease purchase optioning it to me, as an investor, and then I would, in turn, sublease it to the tenants.

Helen: That's possible, I suppose.

Carleton: Or do you think the tenant who's in there right now might want to do that?

notes:

Helen: Well, the tenants originally spoke to the owner about the possibility of buying it, but I don't think they had enough cash. He knows that they like the house and would possibly entertain the idea of working with him. They might even want to do an equity participation or something like that.

Carleton: Sure, that sounds very interesting. Let me also ask you one last question. As a real estate investor yourself, you know that it's important to be able to buy properties and have them make economic sense. One of the ways to do that is to put as little as possible down on them, and this property sounds very attractive from that standpoint. Do you think that you might be willing to take a portion of your commission in the form of a note?

Helen: That shouldn't be a problem. Also, just to let you know, we do specialize in FHA and VA repossessed properties. I didn't know if you knew about those types of houses available for sale.

Carleton: Thank you for mentioning that. I am aware of them, yes. I tell you what; let me drive by and take a look at the property, and if I decide I want to see it, then I'll get back in touch with you.

Helen: Okay, and if you're interested in knowing what's available under the HUD and the VA repossession list, which are generally good buys because they're more below market value, give us a call back. Also, if you want us to put you on our mailing list, we'll send out the list to you, so that you'll have access to those properties.

Carleton: Well, for the moment I don't want to burden you with any more mailings than you already have. But let me look at this property and get back to you. May I ask what the address of the property is?

Helen: It's at 1234 Main Street.

Carleton: You've been so nice. Thank you a lot for your time.

Helen: You're quite welcome, Carleton.

Carleton: Bye-bye.

Call Summary

This property might be an attractive investment. The seller is flexible, the broker is willing to assist in financing by taking a note for the commission, and the property is occupied by a long-term tenant who is pleased to be living in the home and might consider a lease option arrangement. At first glance, it appears that the property might provide a positive cash flow, especially if it can be bought with no down payment. In short, the matter is well worth pursuing.

Eileen—Seller Facing Foreclosure

Background

Eileen and her husband are owners who are facing foreclosure on a three-bedroom, single-family home. The newspaper ad that prompted my call reads as follows:

> FACING FORECLOSURE
> MUST SELL. TWO LOTS, 3BR, 2BA, LG LIVING ROOM
> & KITCHEN. DINING RM, GARAGE, SHED, PATIO,
> FANS, AIR CONDITIONING AND HEAT. FENCED
> YARD. CLOSE TO SCHOOLS AND SHOPPING. $78,000.
> 555-5555

Telephone Conversation

Eileen: Hello?

Carleton: Hi, I'm calling about your ad in the newspaper—the two lots, three-bedroom, two-bath home.

Eileen: Yes?

Carleton: My name is Carleton. May I ask your first name?

Eileen: Eileen.

Carleton: Eileen, could you tell me a little bit about the home?

Eileen: What do you want to know?

Carleton: For example, what is the square footage of the property?

Eileen: The square footage is 1,391. That's the total living area.

Carleton: Is the property being sold with any appliances?

Eileen: It's got a range, refrigerator, dishwasher, washer, dryer, pump and two filters.

Carleton: I notice it has a garage. Is that a single or a double? Also, there's a shed in the back?

Eileen: Yes, it is a double garage, and we do have a nice-sized shed for our yard equipment.

Carleton: Can you tell me about the financing—by which I mean what existing financing is on the property?

notes:

Eileen: It's with Pacific Company, and it is not assumable.

Carleton: What's the outstanding balance on the mortgage?

Eileen: Right now, it's about $70,000. It's the highest-priced piece of property in the whole neighborhood. I do need to sell it, though. That's why I put the price down.

Carleton: Would you consider a lease option on the property, Eileen?

Eileen: I'll be honest with you. Right now, I'm five months behind on my mortgage payment and that wouldn't help me.

Carleton: No, I can see where it wouldn't. But I appreciate your honesty. My problem is that I'm a real estate investor, and I'm just not able to put new financing on every property I buy.

Eileen: I understand that. Absolutely.

Carleton: So I'm just going to wish you the best of luck in selling.

Eileen: Okay. Well, thank you.

Carleton: And thanks an awful lot for your time.

Eileen: You're welcome.

Carleton: Bye-bye.

Call Summary

At this stage of the game, this property is unattractive from an investment standpoint. The mortgage cannot be assumed and is five months behind in payments, and the seller is inflexible. However, due to the fact that two extra lots are included with the property, it might be worth pursuing this lead once the lender takes the property back as an REO. If the mortgage were assumable, it might be worth buying the property for the amount of the back payments and giving the sellers a modest amount of cash for any equity they have in the property.

Dick—Owner of a Home With Rental Units

Background

Dick is the owner of a three-bedroom, single-family home with two unattached apartments. The Internet listing that prompted my call reads as follows:

> IMMACULATE 3 BR, 2 BA HOME PLUS TWO 1 BR APARTMENTS WITH $730 PER MONTH INCOME. HOLLOW TILE CONSTRUCTION. ALL NEW KITCHENS AND BATHS. OWNER MOVING. WILL HOLD PARTIAL NOTE FOR EQUITY. ASSUME FHA MORTGAGE. $131,900.

Telephone Conversation

Dick: Hello?

Carleton: Yes, sir. I'm calling about your ad on the Internet for the three-bedroom, two-bath home with two one-bedroom apartments.

Dick: Yes?

Carleton: My name is Carleton. May I ask your first name?

Dick: Yeah, my name is Dick.

Carleton: Well, Dick. Tell me a little bit about the property. For example, have the apartments been in existence since the property was built or are they add-ons?

Dick: No, they've been there since the property was originally built, as far as I know.

Carleton: And you're getting what, about $365 a month for each one?

Dick: Yeah. One is a little smaller than the other. We get $340 for the small one and $390 for the other.

Carleton: Is the property zoned for three units, by the way?

Dick: Yes, it has been for many years.

Carleton: I ask because I'm a real estate investor, and one of the things I run into sometimes when I buy properties where there are two or three units is that some of them have been built on property that is only suitable for single-family residential use.

Dick: Well, I checked before we bought, about five years ago. Went to the courthouse, and in the records, they had it listed for two rentals.

Carleton: Oh, they did?

notes:

Dick: Yes.

Carleton: That's good to hear. Tell me. What appliances are you including with the home and apartments?

Dick: Well, we're actually going to move out of the house fairly soon, and we won't take any appliances with us.

Carleton: And how long have your tenants occupied the apartments?

Dick: The upstairs tenant has been there a year as of last November. The downstairs tenants will have been there three years come April first. We did quite a bit to the apartments when we bought them. The apartments hadn't been updated in years, and I had the tenants move out, and went into the kitchens and bathrooms and had the bathrooms retiled and new cabinets built for the kitchens, and so on.

Carleton: Are the units actually a part of the home or are they separate?

Dick: No, they're in a separate building. The building is about 30 feet in back of the house. The downstairs apartment is about 600 square feet and the upstairs apartment is about 400. That one has stayed rented quite well. My first tenant in there stayed three years.

Carleton: It's a very convenient location.

Dick: It is, yeah.

Carleton: If I may ask—what kind of existing financing do you have? I see it's an FHA assumable mortgage.

Dick: It's in the amount of $113,000 at 11.5%.

Carleton: Which makes your payments what?

Dick: They're $1,201 a month.

Carleton: And that includes principal, interest, taxes, and insurance?

Dick: That's right.

Carleton: And I see you're looking to get equity over and above the mortgage amount of about $18,000 or so. Dick, do you need any cash at closing?

Dick: Yeah, I do. In fact, I won't get involved in a deal with anybody unless they have at least $12,000.

notes:

Carleton: That certainly wouldn't be a problem in my case. But tell me—could you take that $12,000 down payment spread out over a short period of time?

Dick: How short is "short?"

Carleton: Maybe 12 months, 18 months—something like that?

Dick: No. I wouldn't want to do that.

Carleton: I see. But you would be willing to assist in the financing for the balance.

Dick: Yes.

Carleton: And what did you have in mind there? Five years? Ten years?

Dick: I'd rather make it five, if I could. Or get all cash.

Carleton: How long have you had the property on the market?

Dick: I put up a sign about a year ago and didn't worry about it. Then, in the last month, I've been advertising on the Internet.

Carleton: Yeah, that's where I saw it. It sounds like a nice house. Why are you selling, out of curiosity?

Dick: Well, three years ago my wife had a job offer in Melbourne that was just too good for her to pass up, and I was due to retire out of the post office. So I said, what the heck, take it. Work for another ten years. You need something. You know, it was too good.

Carleton: Sure.

Dick: So that's when we decided to move. I know we've messed around for three years now with the property, figuring this way and that way. But we finally bought property and built a house. They're 99% complete now, so we'll be moving in a week or two, maybe.

Carleton: Are there any other renters in your neighborhood that you know of, Dick?

Dick: Oh, yes. Many, if not most.

Carleton: Do many of the houses have apartments that are attached?

Dick: Most of them do. In fact, it's kind of unusual if they don't.

notes:

Carleton: How about the homes themselves? Are some of them rented out?

Dick: Let me think. The one on the corner is a rental. It changed hands recently, and now it's for rent.

Carleton: I was just wondering what renters in your area are paying for three-bedrooms?

Dick: Well, that one is only a two-bedroom, one-bath, and it rented for $550, according to the new owner.

Carleton: So you think yours would rent for more than $550?

Dick: I would certainly think so, yes. Especially since that one is a two-bedroom, one-bath and this one has three bedrooms and two baths—not to mention it's in a lot better shape.

Carleton: How old is the home?

Dick: It was built in 1925. It's got high ceilings, wood floors, ...

Carleton: Would you consider a lease option on the property?

Dick: Yeah, I think we would. It's something that I would have to talk over with my wife, you know, and a lawyer. I don't know that much about lease options.

Carleton: One last question, Dick. Do you have any idea what your annual taxes on that property are?

Dick: $732.

Carleton: $732?

Dick: Yeah. Although, they did go up about $40 this year.

Carleton: Dick, let me do this. It sounds like a very nice place. Let me give it some thought, and if I can schedule a time to come out and take a look at it, if I decide to do that, I'll get back in touch with you.

Dick: Sure thing.

Carleton: And thank you a lot for your time.

Dick: No problem.

Carleton: Bye-bye.

notes:

Call Summary

This property is probably worth pursuing. The seller is anxious to sell so that he can move to another city where a home he is building is almost complete. He demonstrates his flexibility in that he is willing to hold a note for a portion of the purchase price, and is also willing to consider a lease option.

If the home can be rented for $600 per month, the total monthly income will be $1,330 ($600 for the home plus $730 for the apartments)—which is enough to support the current monthly payment of principal, interest, taxes, and insurance. In performing a complete financial analysis of the property, however, it's important to consider that the property taxes might increase from $732 a year to as much as $1,500 a year. The buyer could increase the property income stream by refinancing the loan at a lower rate; however, even at the current rate, the buyer would enjoy a positive cash flow. In this case, it would also be wise to close on the property only when a tenant for the house was found.

REVIEW

Summary

To achieve success as a real estate investor, you must learn to use the telephone to gather information about prospective properties and sellers. Doing so can save you many hours of time that would otherwise be wasted pursuing bad investments.

When you talk to a prospective seller over the telephone, you should always be polite and be a good listener. You should also direct the conversation to gain information about the property, the financing, the seller, and the broker or agent, if one is involved. The *Seller Information Form* included in the *Real Estate Forms Portfolio* will guide you through the call and provide you with an easy way to record and organize the information you obtain.

Questions

- What type of *Seller Information Form* should you keep in an "inflexible" file? (See page 8-2.)

- What are the two rules you should always follow when talking to a prospective seller over the telephone? (See page 8-2.)

- What are the four key types of information you must obtain about a prospective lead? (See page 8-3.)

- Why should you ask the seller what price they'd consider taking if you paid all cash for the property? (See page 8-6.)

- When should you fill out a *Property Analysis Form*? (See page 8-7.)

notes:

ACTION STEPS

1. Search the classified ads in the newspaper or on the Internet and create a contact list of telephone numbers for five properties that might interest you.

2. Make five photocopies of the *Seller Information Form* in the *Real Estate Forms Portfolio*.

3. Call each of the sellers on your contact list, and fill out a *Seller Information Form* for each call.

4. File each *Seller Information Form* as good, flexible, inflexible, or rejected.

5. Transfer the information from your *Seller Information Form* to your *Property Analysis Form* if you intend to visit the property.

FINAL COMMENTS

Gathering information over the telephone is part of the numbers game of finding properties and flexible sellers. To be successful, you must keep in mind that for every 25 telephone contacts you make, you might find only four or five properties worth inspecting. Of those properties, you might make offers on only two or three, and perhaps only purchase one. However, if your goal is to purchase only one property per year, it might take only 25 calls to do the trick!

VALUATION

*"When someone **purchases** a home to live in, their decision making is heavily affected by emotion. The same can be said for a person **selling** a home.*

*As a real estate investor, you cannot let **emotion** play a part in your **decision making**, and rely on information coming from a property owner, who is giving you their "best-guess" estimates about neighborhood property **prices** and rent rates.*

*Before you buy any **property**, you need to know its true market value, based on what other similar properties have sold for, the rental income it will **generate**, and all the costs of **ownership**."*

 *Carleton Sheets*

9

DETERMINING THE VALUE OF INVESTMENT PROPERTY

Before you purchase an investment property, you should always perform a "common sense" financial analysis to ensure that you're going to make money on the transaction. The analysis should take into account the value of the property and its expected cash flow as an income producer. To correctly analyze the property value and cash flow for an investment property, you need to know what to look for and how to run the numbers.

In this chapter, you will learn:

- What factors influence property value.

- What to look for when you inspect a property.

- The fundamentals of three approaches to determining property value.

- How to perform a cash flow analysis using the *Cash Flow Analysis* form provided in the *Real Estate Forms Portfolio*.

When you complete this chapter, you will be able to:

- Determine the value of investment properties in your area.

- Use the *Cash Flow Analysis* form, *Market Sales Analysis* form and *Buyer's Property Inspection Report* in the *Real Estate Forms Portfolio*.

THE INEXACT NATURE OF VALUE

It would be easy to determine the value of any item or product if that item or product was bought and sold in a perfect marketplace. It goes without saying, however, that there is no such thing as a perfect marketplace. The stock market is about as close as we get to perfect, because at any given moment, you can know a stock's exact selling price and can make a judgment to buy or sell at that price. Real estate is on the other end of the spectrum—not only because no two properties are alike, but also because many sellers ask whatever they think their property is worth, and many buyers base what they'll pay on their emotional response to the property.

To figure out whether you're going to make money on a real estate investment, you must first determine the value of the property you're buying. To determine the value, you need to know what factors influence property value—and why.

> *"Many sellers ask whatever price they believe their property is worth. Many buyers will pay a price for a property in direct relationship to the property's ability to satisfy their emotional needs."*

WHAT DETERMINES PROPERTY VALUE

To succeed as a real estate investor, you must possess a thorough knowledge of the marketplace, especially when it comes to property value. In particular, you have to be aware of the factors impacting value. You must also be aware that only some of the factors are objective and measurable. Others are subjective and depend strongly on the emotions of the parties involved.

Objective Factors
The objective factors that influence the value of a property include things like the condition of the property, its location, size, market demand, and financing. A good investor is capable of making these basic property observations on his or her own. However, other factors should be taken into account when you perform a cash flow analysis on the property.

Subjective Factors
Subjective factors are more difficult to quantify than objective factors and may require more thorough investigation to uncover. Part of what makes the real estate market imperfect is that emotions are often involved. Many sellers ask whatever price they believe their property is worth, and many buyers are willing

notes:

to pay a price for a property based not on its value, but on its ability to satisfy their emotional needs. Generally speaking, investment-motivated purchases are affected less by emotion than are personal purchases. To a sophisticated investor, emotion plays only a very small part in determining the value of a 500,000-square-foot office building, but emotion plays a major part in the purchase of a home to live in by a typical homebuyer.

As an investor, it's important to keep your emotional needs in check and to concentrate on your financial needs. You cannot afford to fall in love with a property. Your sole concern should be how well the property under consideration will benefit you financially once you acquire it.

At some point, you might find yourself competing with other prospective purchasers who are evaluating a property with a heavy emotional bias. In such a case, the emotional biases of your competitors will probably make them pay a higher price for the property than your financial analysis tells you it's worth. If that happens, be patient and move on to the next property. Only when you acquire a property based on its value as determined by a financial analysis will you make a profit.

HOW TO INSPECT A PROPERTY

For the most part, inspecting requires common sense observations. While you might not be a builder or an architect or be able to read a blueprint, you can probably walk, crawl, and see. Consequently, you should at least try to visually spot potential problem areas—such as those that might detract from the overall value of the property and add to the cost of repairs and maintenance. If you identify suspected problems, you might determine that you should use the professional services of a licensed property inspector, builder, or architect, or even move on to another property.

> *"Common sense and personal observations are both important when inspecting properties and making purchase decisions."*

In general, you should make it your practice to systematically and completely inspect the exterior and interior of the property. The *Buyer's Property Inspection Report* included in the *Real Estate Forms Portfolio* provides an excellent checklist to use for evaluating both areas of the property. Table 9.1 lists some items of particular importance to look for:

Table 9.1: Things to Look for When Inspecting a Property

Area	What to Look For
Exterior	• **Termites and dry rot**—Walk around the outside of the property and look for evidence of termites and dry rot in the wood. • **Foundations**—Look for cracks and for signs that the foundation may have settled. • **Roof**—Look for discolored roof sections or indications that a portion of the roof may need replacing. • **Chimney**—Look to see if mortar is missing from the chimney. If the roof is not accessible, use binoculars to inspect the chimney. • **Septic tank**—If the property has a septic tank, look for lush, green grass on top, which may indicate poor absorption. • **Brick properties**—Check the condition of the mortar; crumbling, missing, or discolored mortar may indicate the building needs to be tuck-pointed.
Interior	• **Water stains**—Be alert for water stains on the walls or ceilings, including closets, or cracks in the wallboard or baseboard. New paint on one ceiling or all the ceilings, but not on the walls, may indicate an attempt to mask a leak. Different colored carpeting in one or two rooms may mean a sale at a local carpet store, or it may mean that the carpet was replaced because of water damage. • **Lead-based paint**—Check that the paint used in the interior was not lead-based. If a seller says that lead-based paint was not used, make sure to include a signed lead-based paint guarantee in the contract. • **Windows**—Look for any evidence of leaks around window frames. Open and close the windows to make sure that they are in operating condition. • **Appliances**—Manually check all appliances, including heating and air conditioning equipment. • **Equipment, electrical systems, and plumbing**—Flush toilets and turn water faucets on to determine if there are leaks or inadequate pressure. Check under bathroom and kitchen cabinets for any evidence of water or water stains.

notes:

• **Radon gas**—Determine whether the basement has a problem with radon gas by calling a service company in your area. (Radon is a radioactive gas caused by the decomposition of materials in the ground and is suspected of causing cancer.)

CALCULATING THE VALUE OF A PROPERTY

When an appraiser determines the value of a property, the value is appraised as of a certain date. This value is not cast in stone—it's only the appraiser's judgment of the value of that property as of the specified date. Furthermore, even though an appraiser determines a single estimate of value, property market values always exist within a range.

Because so many variables are involved in determining the value of a property, appraisers generally try to determine the value in three ways. While you probably won't use a professional appraiser in the purchase of every property, you do need to become familiar with the three different methods that are used. As you read about the three methods, keep in mind that an appraiser always ignores any debt that may be on the property. In other words, an appraiser treats the property as if it were debt-free. This does not yield a complete analysis for your purposes.

> *"If you count all your assets, you'll always show a profit!"*
>
> -Robert Quillen

The three methods of property valuation that you can learn to use are:

• **Market Sales Approach**—Look at the price that similar properties have sold for recently in the same or similar neighborhoods. Make adjustments based on square footage, age, construction, number of bedrooms, and amenities.

• **Reproduction Cost Approach**—Estimate the cost of building the same or similar structure, add the cost of land, and subtract wear and tear (that is, real depreciation).

• **Net Income Approach**—Determine the property value based on its income stream (net operating income).

Appraisers reconcile these approaches and give the most weight to the approach that gives the best evidence of the property value.

Method 1: Market Sales Approach

The market sales approach determines the value of a property by considering the price that similar properties in the same or similar neighborhoods have sold for recently. For smaller properties, such as single-family and two-unit homes, the market sales approach is the most accurate and reliable method of determining value. It's important to focus on the selling price in the analysis because the asking price of a property currently for sale is only someone's estimate of the value of the

notes:

property. For example, the asking price might be a product of a "let's offer it for this price and see what happens" approach.

You should also find out the approximate square footage of each property, as well as the age, construction (for example, cement block, brick, or wood frame), numbers of bedrooms and baths, and any extra amenities the property has, such as a two-car garage, porch, den, central heat and/or air conditioning, or finished basement. The size of the lot can also add to or detract from the value. You can find the property information necessary to make the needed comparisons in your targeted investment area by visiting my website—*www.CarletonSheets.com.* There, you'll be able to access online information about the properties you are investigating.

> *"To perform a market sales approach, you must first make sure you are comparing 'apples to apples.' That is to say, you must take care that the properties you're using for comparison are in the same (or very similar) neighborhood as the property you're analyzing."*

In the case of larger properties, such as apartment buildings and office buildings that produce rental income, you should make your market sales approach comparison based on two factors:

- The selling price per apartment unit (obtained by dividing the selling price by the number of apartments).

- The selling price per square foot (obtained by dividing the selling price by the square footage).

You can obtain most of this information from real estate agents in your local area. To research it on your own, you can search the public records, available in every county, located in the tax assessor's office.

To help you summarize and keep track of such information, I have included a *Market Sales Analysis* form in the *Real Estate Forms Portfolio.* Figure 9.1 shows an example of that form.

MARKET SALES ANALYSIS

SUBJECT PROPERTY

ADDRESS	ROOMS	BDRMS	BATHS	GAR	AGE	STYLE	SQ FT	CONSTRUCTION	AMENITIES	REMARKS
548 White Oak	8	7	2.5	170	21	2-S	2150	Frame	Hardwood Floor, Fireplace	Freshly painted, sharp FR w/FP

PROPERTIES ON MARKET

ADDRESS	ROOMS	BDRMS	BATHS	GAR	AGE	STYLE	SQ FT	CONSTRUCTION	AMENITIES	LIST PRICE	DAYS ON MKT	REMARKS
555 Redwood	8	4	2.5	2	25	2-S	2250	Frame	Drapes, Fireplace	85,000	60	Poor condition
1108 Pinecrest	8	3	2	2.5	20	RR	1950	Frame	Water Softner, Appliances, New Rof	85,900	30	Sharp home

PROPERTIES SOLD

ADDRESS	ROOMS	BDRMS	BATHS	GAR	AGE	STYLE	SQ FT	CONSTRUCTION	AMENITIES	LIST PRICE	DAYS ON MKT	SALE DATE	SALE PRICE
346 Evergreen	9	4	2.5	2.5	23	2-S	2275	Frame	All appliances	79,900	78	9-1	78,000
493 Rockhurst	7	4	2.5	1	23	2-S	2025	Frame	pool table, lawn equip.	78,900	92	10-28	78,900
190 Seabury	7	4	2.5	1.5	24	2-S	2075	Frame	New Furnace	81,900	55	7-13	79,000
213 Thornhurst	8	4	2.5	1.5	24	2-S	2180	Frame	Fireplace, appliances	84,400	97	11-7	82,842

PROPERTIES EXPIRED/CANCELLED

ADDRESS	ROOMS	BDRMS	BATHS	GAR	AGE	STYLE	SQ FT	CONSTRUCTION	AMENITIES	LIST PRICE	DAYS ON MKT	REMARKS
417 Rockhurst	8	4	2.5	1	28	2-S	1960	Frame	Washer/Dryer			

Recommended Price Range $ 85,000 – 86,900

COMMENTS:

Average of Sold Properties $ 81,275

Average of Properties on Market $ 85,450

Average of Properties Expired/Cancelled $ N/A

Figure 9.1: Example *Market Sales Analysis* Form

reproduction cost approach
—A technique used to evaluate a property by estimating the cost of building the same or similar structure, adding the cost of land and subtracting an allowance for wear and tear.

Method 2: Reproduction Cost Approach

The *reproduction cost approach* (also called the replacement cost approach) takes into account the current cost of building the same or a very similar structure and the cost of land, less any wear and tear the property may show. The first two factors are pretty objective, but the last one is not and can sometimes distort the true value of the property.

Costs of construction are estimated on a per-square-foot or per-cubic-foot basis. Usually, no attempt is made to estimate the actual cost of the construction materials. The easiest way for you to estimate the cost of construction is to refer to a cost manual such as those produced by *Marshall & Swift* ® and *R.S. Means*. These resources are available at major retail chain bookstores or the local library.

To determine the value of the property, simply perform a reproduction cost approach and then add the price that other comparable lots are selling for.

notes:

You can determine driveway and landscaping costs by contacting firms that specialize in these areas or by using the previously mentioned resources. By performing an analysis like this on several properties, you will soon develop a very good perspective on building costs in your area. You can then make some comparisons with the information you developed using the market sales approach. Because of the difficulties in objectively determining a value for wear and tear, however, this appraisal method is the least reliable way of determining value, especially for older properties.

Method 3: Net Income Approach

The *net income approach* is used primarily for evaluating larger income-producing properties—such as those with three units or more. It does not work as well when applied to houses and two-unit properties, because they may be subject to too many emotional factors that can affect the prices in the marketplace.

> *net income approach*—A method used to value income properties based on the net income they produce.

In simple terms, the net income approach says that the value of a property is a function of the net operating income (or net income) it produces. The net operating income is the money that you would earn if you owned the property free and clear of any mortgage debt. If rents increase or expenses decrease, the net income goes up, and so does the value of the property. In short, the greater the net operating income, the higher the value of the property. No matter what the indicated market value of the property, if it does not generate enough net income to pay the mortgage payments and generate some extra spendable cash, you should not buy it.

The net income approach for determining a property's value can have powerful implications. This is especially true if you are able to purchase the property based on its market sales analysis value (the amount that comparable properties have sold for), and sell it for its net income value (the property's value in rela- . tion to the net income it generates before any mortgage payments). For example, not long ago, I purchased a four-unit property that had a net operating income of approximately $10,000 per year. The purchase price for the property was $100,000, but I was able to buy it with a down payment of only $2,500. Over the course of 18 months, I was able to raise the rental income to where the property had a net operating income of $14,000 per year. At this point, I sold the property for $135,000—realizing a $35,000 profit on my initial investment of $2,500. The higher net operating income was responsible for the increase in value.

To witness the power of increasing the net operating income, suppose you purchase a large, fairly new, 200-unit apartment building. (For this example, the actual amount that you pay and the terms are not important.) After buying the property, you raise the rents just $15 per month, which nets an additional $3,000 per month or $36,000 per year in income. From the standpoint of an

notes:

investor looking for a 10% return (assuming no increase in expenses), you have increased the value of the property by $360,000 ($36,000 divided by 10%). Likewise, an immediate monthly decrease in expenses of just $10 per unit could produce an additional increase in value of $240,000! Can you see how owners of large income properties make fortunes?

> *"To suggest that the value of a property might be determined by the financing is a little uncomfortable for many people. This is another traditional belief that a little creative thinking can overcome."*

Whether or not you reveal your use of the net income analysis approach to the seller depends, in part, on whether you're dealing with a small property or a multi-unit property. Many owners of small properties, especially single-family and two-unit properties, have never heard of this method of determining value, and so their prices are out of line with the true investment value of the property. In such cases, you would probably be best advised not to tell the sellers how you arrived at the price you are offering. Instead, you can simply say, "I've done some figuring and this appears to be the best offer I can make now." By wording your response in this open-ended way, you are leaving room for a larger *counteroffer* at a later date if you choose to make one. Sometimes, though, it can be very helpful to let the sellers know that you will be renting the property. You can tell them that based on the rent you expect to receive for the home, and the expenses you expect to incur, your offer is the best that you can do to make economic sense.

counteroffer —Rejection of an offer to buy or sell, with a simultaneous substitute offer.

When purchasing multi-unit properties, however, it's generally a good idea to show the seller how and why your appraisal method indicates that what you are offering is a very objective and realistic price. Doing so establishes your credibility as a buyer of large properties.

PERFORMING A CASH FLOW ANALYSIS

Assume that you have found a four-unit property that you think is a bargain because you have already determined the market value. Even so, the question you have to ask yourself now is, "If I purchase the property for the asking price, can I afford to own it?" To come up with the answer to the question, you need to determine the cash available to make mortgage payments and the after-tax effects of owning an income property. To determine the cash available to you to make mortgage payments from an income property, you should use the *Cash Flow Analysis* form (see Figure 9.2) included in the *Real Estate Forms Portfolio*.

CASH FLOW ANALYSIS

1. Gross Income:

1.A. Estimated Annual Gross	$33,600 (4 x $700 x 12)	
1.B. Other Income		
1.C. Total Gross Income		$33,600
1.D. Less Vacancy Allowance		$1,500
1.E. Effective Gross Income		$32,100

2. Expenses:

2.A. Taxes	$3,300	
Insurance	$1,000	
Water/Sewer	$0	
Garbage	$600	
Electricity	$200	
Licenses	$0	
2.B. Advertising	$300	
Supplies	$100	
2.C. Maintenance	$2,160	
Snow Removal	$0	
Pest Control	$0	
Management (Off-Site)	$0	
Management (On-Site)	$0	
Accounting/Legal	$200	
2.D. Miscellaneous	$2800	
2.E. Total Expenses		$10,660
2.F. Net Operating Income		$21,440

3. Debt Service:

1st Mortgage	To be Determined	
2nd Mortgage		
3rd Mortgage		
Total Debt Service		

4. Cash Flow: To be Determined

Figure 9.2: Example *Cash Flow Analysis* Form

notes:

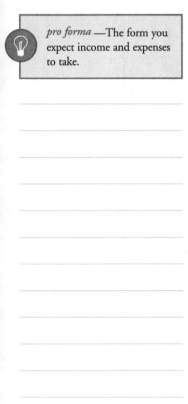

> **debt service** —The sum of the annual principal and interest payments made on a loan.

> **Effective Gross Income (EGI)** —Estimated annual gross income and other income less a vacancy allowance.

> **pro forma** —The form you expect income and expenses to take.

The *Cash Flow Analysis* form is divided into four major sections:

1. Gross Income
2. Expenses
3. *Debt Service* (the annual mortgage payments on the property)
4. Cash Flow

Each section includes various subsections that itemize the monetary intake and outflow that determines overall cash flow. The following list provides more details concerning what factors play into each section:

1. Gross Income

This section is where you calculate the *Effective Gross Income (EGI)*.

1.A. Estimated Annual Gross Income
Apartment Building

If the property you are analyzing is an apartment building, remember to construct a "theoretical" *pro forma*, that is, what you expect income and expenses to be. You should do this because it is not uncommon to find a 15% to 20% variation in the rents in apartment buildings.

In some cases, an expenditure of money may be necessary to bring low income producing units up to the condition of the highest income producing units. In still other cases, money may have to be spent rehabbing all the units to make them comparable to competitive rental units in other buildings. For this reason, your theoretical pro forma may show considerably more net operating income than is shown in the owner's tax return. On the other hand, if the units are all rented at the top of the rent range, but the seller is managing the property (thus not paying a management fee), the pro forma may actually be lower than the net income reported by the owner in the individual's personal tax return.

The purchase price offered should be based on the property's effective gross income (less expenses). The effective gross income may be determined by examining the property's rent roll. Along with this information, the owner's previous tax returns will enable you to construct a "theoretical" pro forma. In some cases, owners are reluctant to raise the rent of a long-term or elderly tenant—thus keeping rents below market. In other cases, some units may be physically inferior. Calculate the gross income as if all apartments were renting for the amount received under the terms of the highest paying lease for the same type of unit—if that lease represents a reasonable fair market rent rate that you feel you will be able to charge. Only if you are sure the rents are below market, and you intend to raise them, should you use the new higher rents in your calculations.

If any cost is required to bring a below-average apartment unit up to the level of other units, include this cost in a separate cash requirement analysis and use the *Buyer's Property Inspection Report* in the *Real Estate Forms Portfolio* to determine the cost.

Rented Single-Family House

To analyze a rented, single-family house, use the same approach as you would for an apartment building. If you are living in the house and intend to rent it, your gross income figure comes from analyzing the amount for which other comparable houses in the area are renting. Ideally, a single-family home should generate, at a minimum, a monthly income between 1% and 1.3% of what you would pay for the property to support a 100% financed no money down transaction. For example, a $150,000 home you are considering acquiring should be rentable in the $1,500 to $2,000 per month range for you to generate a positive cash flow, and finance 100% of the purchase price at fair market interest rates. If the fair market rent for the house is less than $1,500, you either need to use below-market-rate seller financing, defer a portion of the purchase price, or pass on the house and go on to the next property.

1.B. Other Income

Other income represents income that might come from coin-operated equipment, such as washers and dryers, a pay telephone, soft drink vending machines, electronic games, or a pool table (in larger apartment buildings).

1.C. Total Gross Income

This value represents the sum of the Estimated Gross Income and Other Income.

1.D. Vacancy Allowance

This value represents a vacancy rate and collection loss. In a competitive single-family home rental market, this allowance might reasonably be 4% to 6% of your *gross income* (multi-unit vacancy rates may be higher, depending on the area). This would allow for 15 to 20 vacant days per year, per apartment unit or home. Keep in mind that forfeited deposits usually offset collection losses in most cases. Since in some areas it may be higher, your research in this area becomes important.

gross income —The total income from a property before the deduction of expenses.

1.E. Effective Gross Income

This value represents the result of subtracting the Vacancy Allowance from the Total Gross Income.

2. Expenses

You can complete the expense portion of this form by looking at the owner's records and tax return—which you should always request to examine before closing. (What you are requesting is only the one page, "Schedule E," from the owner's most recent income tax return. Schedule E reports taxable income and expenses for a particular property.) A good purchase contract makes the purchase subject to the buyer verifying all income and expense data—which is why such a clause is included in the *Real Estate Purchase Contract* included in the *Real Estate Forms Portfolio*.

When you look at the seller's records, be careful that you do not compare the expenses for last year with your income estimate for next year. If you do this,

notes:

you will arrive at an incorrect figure, and the mistake could result in the difference between a positive cash flow and a negative cash flow. You may also have to adjust the expense data you receive from the seller since expenses go up each year, mostly due to inflation. There is usually no reason that a transfer of ownership changes the cost of utilities. For insurance, however, you might be able to locate a more favorable insurance quote for the same coverage in order to save on expenses.

2.A. Taxes

Real estate taxes represent one of the most underestimated costs of ownership. Many times, taxes are increased with a change of ownership because the tax assessor's office uses the new selling price as a basis for determining the tax value. Determining the general relationship between taxes and the selling price in your area will help you estimate taxes. You can do this by talking with the tax assessor's office personnel or by accessing that information at *www.CarletonSheets.com*. You can even make this determination yourself by looking at the percentage of taxes compared to the selling price of properties that have been sold in the last several years. You might find that real estate taxes will average 1% to 2% (even more in some areas) of the total selling price of a property. Use this as a guide in calculating estimated taxes for the property under consideration.

2.B. Advertising

When you have a vacancy, advertising the property is often necessary. Where, how, and when (which day) you advertise plays an important part in determining your advertising expenses—as does the size and type of ad. Consult your local newspapers for current pricing information.

2.C. Maintenance

Maintenance and repairs are difficult to accurately assess. Such costs vary because of such diverse factors as the amount of deferred maintenance, climate, construction, age, and the cost of local labor. The owner's records are of some help in arriving at a realistic estimate, although it would be a rare owner who would be totally candid in sharing the complete maintenance and repair expense records. Again, this is why it is so important to examine the owner's Schedule E. Other experienced investors in your area might also provide you with guidance in determining your anticipated expenses.

In many cases, owners of small properties do their own maintenance. Since you might want to have your maintenance done by outside contractors (which will leave you more time for investing), you should take this into consideration.

A good rule of thumb is to budget maintenance costs as follows (these figures might be affected by all the variables already mentioned):

- Condominium—$30 to $40 per month per unit
- Single-family home—$50 to $60 per month
- Multi-unit building—$40 to $55 per month per unit

notes:

This is why you will probably be managing the properties yourself, especially if it's an early purchase. You should still provide a management fee for yourself at the going market rate, which can be easily determined by calling several management companies in the area. Even though you won't actually pay yourself a management fee, and will not be able to deduct this as if you were actually paying an outside firm, it will give you a greater cash flow at the end of the year. Plus, anytime you do decide to turn to an outside management firm, the money will be there.

2.D. Miscellaneous

This category might be better titled, "Miscellaneous Surprises and Mistakes." To figure out how much to add on this line, come up with an amount to cover all the expenses that you might have overlooked or underestimated when you were doing your analysis. A good guide might be to arrive at what you think is a reasonable figure, then double it!

2.E. Total Expenses

To arrive at this total, add all of the expenses on the form. (Although using formulas to estimate your expenses can be misleading and dangerous—to a novice investor, they can sometimes provide a little comfort.) Generally, the following applies to total expense figures based on percentages of effective gross income:

- Single-family homes—20% to 30%
- Six or more units—38% to 50%

The total expense figure for residential properties, six units and larger, should probably be in the range of 38% to 45% of the effective gross income in temperate areas of the country, and 43% to 50% in colder climates. These percentages can be significantly affected, to the extent that tenants pay for their own utilities and maintenance costs, as specified in the lease.

As a landlord, you can charge higher rents if you pay all of the tenants' utilities, but your expenses (and thus your expense percentage) are correspondingly higher. For single-family homes, the expense figure probably runs 20% to 30% regardless of the part of the country where the property is located. Also, for single-family homes, it is very common to have the tenant pay all of his or her utilities.

2.F. Net Operating Income

The result of adding all the expenses and subtracting the total from the Effective Gross Income is *Net Operating Income (NOI)*—also referred to as net income. In effect, NOI is your available budget for debt payments. If you own the property free and clear with no debt, this is your spendable cash flow.

3. Debt Service

Debt service and *servicing the debt* are terms used to describe the annual principal and interest payments, if any, that are made on an outstanding debt

Net Operating Income (NOI)—The balance of cash remaining after deducting the operating expenses of a property from the gross income generated by the property. (Expenses excluded are mortgage principal, interest payments, and depreciation deductions.)

servicing the debt—The act of paying the periodic principal and interest payments on an outstanding obligation.

notes:

obligation. While it would be foolish to ignore the total amount of money that you borrow relative to the value of a property, of primary importance to an investor is what is known as the debt service constant. A debt service constant is the total of 12 monthly principal and interest payments as a percentage of the amount owed.

For example, assume you are purchasing a property with an old 8% mortgage. The original amount of the mortgage was $150,000 with monthly payments of $1,140 per month. The payments are still $1,140 per month, but the loan has been reduced to a present balance of $48,000. The sum of the yearly payments is $13,680—which represents a debt service constant of a whopping 28.5% of the outstanding balance of the loan ($13,680 divided by $48,000).

Given your needs and goals, putting a new mortgage on the property may be advisable, even if it means paying a higher interest rate. Although the interest rate is higher, the monthly payments might be lower. In other words, the current annual payment of $13,680 should cover the mortgage payment on a loan amount that is much greater than $48,000. It might be possible to renegotiate the mortgage and obtain a *blended interest rate* to accomplish the same result.

> *blended interest rate* —The weighted value of two or more interest rates.

The Net Operating Income should be sufficient to cover all the debt service payments with some remaining cash flow. That figure should be covered by the Net Operating Income.

4. Cash Flow

If you do not have enough Net Operating Income to cover the Total Debt Service, you have a negative cash flow—or as I said earlier, an alligator. That means you would have to supply your own cash to supplement what the property does not generate in income. Negative cash flow is not necessarily a bad thing if you can afford it or if it is only temporary. You may still have an excellent investment. Negative cash flow is only bad if it comes as a surprise, and you cannot afford the extra cash out-of-pocket.

If you find a bargain property, you should ask yourself, "Can I afford the existing debt service on the property plus any new debt that I would be putting on the property when I acquire it?" If not, even though the property may be a bargain, do not buy it—that is, unless you are willing to go into your pocket each month or year to feed this alligator.

THE EFFECT OF FINANCING ON PROPERTY VALUE

Many of us are programmed to believe that any product has a determinable value, and if you don't pay cash for it, financing is just something to be worked out. Even professional appraisers suggest a specific value after evaluating a property. Consequently, the suggestion that the value of a product might be determined by the financing is a little uncomfortable for many people. Fortunately, this is another traditional belief that a little creative thinking can overcome.

By understanding that the determination of a property's market value goes hand-in-hand with the financing of that property, you can design terms that allow you to buy according to your individual needs and assets. Where others simply say, "I can't afford it," a whole new world of creative real estate investing awaits you. As we know, even a sophisticated real estate investor or appraiser cannot determine a precise dollar value for a given property. There is a general acceptable market value range, usually plus or minus 2.5%, for every property. But for creative real estate investors, based on the financing available, there could be substantial differences beyond this range.

As an example of the effect of financing on value, assume that two properties—A and B—are physically identical in every respect, that each one is owned free and clear of any mortgages, and an experienced investor has determined that each property has a market value range of between $146,250 and $153,750 (i.e., approximately $150,000). The question here is, "Must the properties necessarily sell for the same price?" The answer is no—due to possible differences in the financing on each property.

First, let's assume that the seller of Property A is asking all cash. Presumably, this means that any buyer has to place a new, relatively high-interest mortgage on the property or have a lot of cash available for the purchase. Factors that will determine whether a buyer can purchase the property will include the size of his or her bank account, the quality of his or her credit, the existence of a large income, and/or an ability and willingness to make large monthly payments.

Now, let's assume that Property B is available with no down payment and low-interest seller financing with little or no qualifying. A prospective purchaser doesn't have to have a large amount of cash, good credit, or an ability to make large mortgage payments. Are both properties identical in value now? Obviously, they are not. This example illustrates that the terms of sale and type of financing can have an enormous effect on the value of a property.

Even though the range of value for Property A is $146,250 to $153,750, it's quite reasonable to expect that the seller might be willing to sell it for $135,000 to $150,000 to a buyer who pays all cash. Let's assume, for the sake of contrast, that the seller of Property B would be willing to accept no money down and take back a *promissory note* and mortgage for the entire amount with little or no interest for three years, and then charge interest only at 6% for another seven years. Because the buyer would be paying interest on the principal only after the property is generating rental income and supporting itself, he or she might be willing to pay $160,000 to $165,000 for Property B. Again, the financing has a direct effect on the value of the property.

promissory note —Written evidence of a debt including the amount, interest rate, and term.

notes:

> *deed*—An instrument conveying title to real property. It usually must be signed by the grantor (seller), and recorded.

Depending on your individual situation, either deal might be right for you as the buyer. In this instance, you can see that the $35,000 difference in value represents a difference of nearly 25%, which is a tremendous variance. To further illustrate this point, assume that I have $150,000 in my left hand and a *deed* to a $150,000 free-and-clear home in my right hand. Which hand holds the commodity with the greatest value? If you guessed they were both equal, you would be wrong. Not everyone would be interested in buying my $150,000 home for $150,000, but with my $150,000 cash I can buy any $150,000 home, many $170,000 homes, and maybe even some $180,000 homes for all cash. The lesson here is that cash is "king" and is the medium of exchange to which every financial alternative is compared.

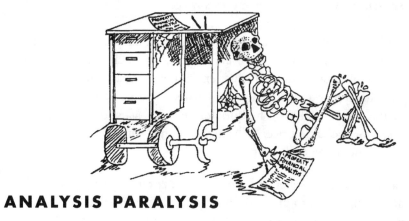

ANALYSIS PARALYSIS

One final thought should be considered when determining the value of a property and its price range. If you spend too much time in analyzing and re-analyzing every property, you will never make an offer and will certainly never purchase a property. This is called "analysis paralysis." Don't wait for that perfect house or investment property. It does not exist!

Examine the property's market value, analyze the potential cash flow, and choose the creative financing techniques that will determine the price you will offer. Then, quickly make a decision to buy it—or move on to another property.

REVIEW
Summary
Many factors affect the value of a property—some are objective and measurable, others are not. To correctly determine the value of a property, you must always keep emotions in check and focus solely on how well a property will benefit you financially—based on your individual needs and assets.

Before you consider buying a property, you should always thoroughly inspect it to determine its physical condition. The inspection should reveal any major defects or repairs that you might need to address should you decide to buy the property.

notes:

Depending on the property and your personal situation, you can use any of three different appraisal methods to determine the value of a property. Each method—market sales approach, reproduction cost approach, or net income approach—takes different factors into account when determining property value.

When deciding whether or not to purchase an income property, it's important to determine if owning the property will result in a positive or negative cash flow. To determine the cash flow potential, you should use the *Cash Flow Analysis* form to itemize the income and the expenses for the property. You should also take into account the fact that financing can greatly affect a property's value.

Questions

- How does emotion affect the value of a property? (See page 9-1.)

- When inspecting a property, what are some of the key conditions to look for? (See page 9-3.)

- Which appraisal method is the most accurate and reliable for single-family dwellings? (See page 9-4.)

- Which appraisal method is the least reliable appraisal method, especially for older properties? (See page 9-6.)

- Which appraisal method should you use for larger (three units or more) residential income properties? (See page 9-7.)

- What does a cash flow analysis tell you about an income property? (See page 9-8.)

- Which is better and why—$150,000 cash or a deed for a property worth $150,000? (See page 9-16.)

ACTION STEPS

Knowledge of your specific real estate marketplace is important to evaluating property values in your area.

1. Contact a real estate agent or use the Internet to research comparable properties in your area. You can go to *www.CarletonSheets.com* for useful tools and resources.

2. Contact a local builder to get an idea of building and land costs for different types of property.

notes:

3. Fill out the *Buyer's Property Inspection Report* on your current residence as if you were going to purchase it.

4. Using the mortgage amortization chart on the back of the *Creative Options Guide* that is included in your literature album, compute the monthly payment for a $150,000 loan at 7%—amortized over thirty years. (Hint: you'll need to multiply the answer on the chart by $150.)

FINAL COMMENTS

Money in real estate is primarily made when you buy, not when you sell. To succeed as a real estate investor, you must learn what determines property value and how to make that knowledge work in your favor. Furthermore, you cannot afford to fall in love with a property. If it doesn't make sense for your bottom line, you must pass and move on. Letting emotions come into play in your real estate investment decisions will only bring you grief (and financial loss). Finally, you need to understand how financing affects the value of a property—if you do, you'll be miles ahead of the many investors who don't. And always remember that, when it comes to value, cash is king!

ADDITIONAL INFORMATION AND RESOURCES

Books to Read

- *Marshall & Swift Reproduction Cost Guide*
911 Wilshire Boulevard, 16th Floor
Los Angeles, CA 90017
(800) 544-2678

- *R.S. Means Construction Costs Data Books*
R.S. Means Company, Inc.
63 Smiths Lane
Kingston, MA 02364-0800
(800) 334-3509

Websites to Visit

- *www.CarletonSheets.com* —Where you can get an online estimate of value of an average unit in a particular price range and geographic area.

DEVELOP

"Throughout my **career**, it has given me a lot of **pleasure,** as well as a sense of pride, to develop new creative financing techniques to **buy property**.

You too can **develop** your own unique **creative financing techniques**. To do this though, you must have a **thorough understanding** of the purchasing situation—that involves yourself, the property, and the seller.

Having done this, **identify** which one of the more than 16 creative financing sources is **appropriate**, then use or create the **technique** that will work best."

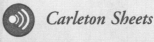 *Carleton Sheets*

10

DEVELOPING CREATIVE FINANCING TECHNIQUES

The secret to succeeding as a real estate investor is to recognize opportunities and apply creative solutions. Creative financing is an essential tool for capitalizing on real estate investment opportunities.

To develop the appropriate creative financing technique, you must assess the situation, locate one or more creative financing sources, and develop a strategy. Creative financing sources can include everything from the seller to home equity loans, from dead assets to government programs, and from partners to private investors. Each strategy is unique to the situation and the financing sources involved.

In this chapter, you will learn:

- How creative financing techniques can make it possible for you to buy real estate with little or no money down.

- How to develop creative financing techniques by using my course.

When you complete this chapter, you will be able to:

- Develop your own creative financing techniques for use in any given situation.

- Analyze the fundamental elements of a real estate transaction (that is, the buyer, the seller, and the property).

- Recognize and understand fundamental real estate finance and purchase concepts.

- Use the *Creative Options Guide* included in your literature album.

notes:

THE IMPORTANCE OF LEVERAGE

As I mentioned in Chapter 2, *Succeeding As a Real Estate Investor,* leverage (using a small amount of money or value to secure a larger value) is the key to creative real estate investing. Leverage is a term that means getting a little to do a lot. In real estate investing, leverage involves the use of other people's money (OPM). For many years, sophisticated real estate investors have used leverage and creative financing techniques to buy property.

CREATIVE FINANCING

Most people think there is only one way for the average person to finance a real estate purchase—that is, go to an institutional lender, like a bank, mortgage company, or savings and loan, and obtain a mortgage. If that were the only way to buy real estate, it would be very difficult to make money as a real estate investor—fortunately, it's not!

To be successful as an investor, you must think creatively and consider the wide range of possibilities that are open to you, such as borrowing money for a down payment from the real estate broker or agent who is helping to arrange your purchase (yes, you really can do that), or using the equity in property you already own as collateral against a loan that you'll use to make a down payment.

The fact is that there are far more creative techniques than there are conventional techniques for financing a real estate purchase. However, to make use of them you have to know what information to look for and what to do with the information when you find it. In short, you have to know how to develop your own technique.

HOW TO DEVELOP A CREATIVE FINANCING TECHNIQUE

Later in the chapter you will learn that there are 16 ingredients—which I will refer to under the *Creative Sources* section—that go individually or in a group of two or more into developing a creative financing technique. Just as there may be eight ingredients in a cake, the way you combine them, and the amount of each ingredient used will produce a different cake each time. In this way, we can say you are developing your own cake recipe. So it is with the 16 ingredients that go into the creative financing purchase of real estate. You are the one creating the financing technique and anyone can do it! All it takes is the willingness to gather as much information as you can; the wisdom to correctly evaluate that information; the open-mindedness to consider unconventional financing options; and

notes:

the imagination to envision, from all those factors, a method of making the transaction work.

To make things simple, you should think of the process of inventing a technique in terms of the "Three S's"—Situation, Source(s), and Strategy. In other words, to develop your own technique, you need to do three things:

- Assess the situation
- Identify financing sources
- Develop a strategy

As you will see shortly, it is not difficult to assess the situation—you just have to be thorough in your thinking and gather all the information you can. Identifying a financing source is not usually difficult, either—and it gets easier the more experienced you become at developing and using my techniques. Developing a strategy takes some creative thinking, but much of it involves combining a small set of basic strategies that I describe in this chapter.

> *"In order to be a creative investor, you must be open-minded and willing to view situations from various perspectives."*

Assessing the Situation

To assess the situation for a potential real estate purchase, you need to have information—lots of it. When you think you have enough, look for more. Only when you've exhausted all of your sources will you be ready to sit down and figure out who wants and needs what. Unfortunately, it is sometimes difficult to find all the information you need. This is particularly true when you are working with real estate brokers or agents who have a listing on a property. They will frequently discourage or even prevent direct contact with the seller.

You cannot rely on real estate brokers or agents to voluntarily disclose the seller's personal information or the property's financial information. Many agents won't consider this information to be relevant to your offer amount or purchase decision. In other situations, it may be a breach of the agent's fiduciary responsibility to the seller to disclose information. I have often seen agents' listing sheets that are devoid of any information concerning the mortgage. When I have questioned the agents about this, they have usually responded by telling me that the mortgage is not assumable. Even though a mortgage might not be assumable, the amount of equity that a seller has in the property is an important part of the information gathering process. You must do whatever you can to obtain this information and any other information concerning the seller's situation that would be important to you in making an offer.

There are really three aspects to assessing the situation for any real estate transaction—the property, the buyer, and the seller. Any or all of the three can give you clues as to which financing source or sources you might be able to use and which strategy you should employ. So, to fully evaluate the situation, you must find out certain information about all three.

The Property Situation
The property situation is largely defined by the condition of the property, its value, and its financial situation (the status of any current financing). A lot of that information can be obtained in public records and by talking to the owner and/or real estate broker or agent, if one is involved.

In the event you are concerned that the transaction will trigger a "*due on sale clause*" in the existing mortgage, you must be prepared to accept the consequences of the entire loan amount being declared due and payable. I strongly recommend you consult an attorney in your state when confronted with this issue and the potential consequences. In any event, you have many avenues to pursue.

> *due on sale clause* —A provision in a mortgage that states the loan is due upon the sale of the property.

The first and most logical option is to go to the present lender and attempt to negotiate an assumption (some of the creative techniques involve the assumption of existing financing) and/or modification of the existing loan. You could even request a new mortgage loan to pay off the existing one. The next option might be to find another institutional or private lender, or even an equity partner. However, there are several other creative financing options that you can explore.

My website—*www.CarletonSheets.com*—provides a vast amount of information about properties all over the country. Not only can you get summaries of public records about a particular property, you can obtain a computerized analysis of the property's worth based on the same principles that appraisers use—all with the click of a mouse button!

Regardless of where you obtain the information, the main questions you need to answer are these:

- Is the property location a handicap or asset?
- What is the physical condition of the property? What repairs or improvements are necessary?
- Are any "extras" included in the property sale—for example, an extra lot, furniture, appliances, or an automobile?
- What is the property layout? Is it functional or does it suffer from *functional obsolescence*?
- What is the offering price of the property, relative to its value, as determined from a survey of comparable property sales?
- If you buy the property, what credits will you receive at closing?

> *functional obsolescence* — Design features that diminish a property's utility and consequently, its value.

notes:

- Is there a broker involved in the sale, or is it a for-sale-by-owner (FSBO) property?
- Are any of the mortgages assumable?
- If the property is rented, how do the rents compare to the true market rent?
- Are there unpaid taxes, special assessments, or other liens?
- What is the interest rate or blended interest rate, if applicable?

The blended interest rate can be estimated by adding the interest costs (in dollars) on all mortgages on the property and dividing the sum by the total amount of the mortgages. For example, assume that you are looking at a property that is on the market for $150,000. There is an existing first mortgage for $80,000 at 8% interest, and a second mortgage of $70,000 at 11% interest. The total yearly interest costs for the two mortgages are $6,400 (8% of $80,000) and $7,700 (11% of $70,000)—the sum of which is $14,100. The total amount of the mortgages is $150,000 ($80,000 plus $70,000). Therefore, the blended interest rate is 9.4% ($14,100 divided by $150,000). Learning the blended rate might encourage you to not reject a property just because it appears to have an unusually high second mortgage interest rate.

Your Situation As the Buyer

You can't make an informed assessment of a real estate transaction without knowing your own situation. While this sounds simplistic, there are many people who do not know their own situation other than superficially. They do not know, for example, exactly how much they could borrow at a bank or the specifics of their credit situation. Saying that your credit is bad or good is not enough; you need to know exactly what it is. You should also know the amount of equity you have in real or *personal property* that you own, or in *dead assets*, like a *time-share* condominium, a boat, or a vacant lot. You should know the amount of equity you have in real estate and the value of securities that you own. All these things are components of your net worth. Do you know if your life insurance policy has a cash value and, if so, the amount? If you don't, you should. Do you know people who would give you money for a solid real estate investment if one were presented to them? Finally, you should know where you stand with respect to any potential partners you might have.

The Seller's Situation

To accurately assess the seller's situation, you need to know certain things about the seller. For example:

- Where will the seller go after the property is sold (if owner occupied)?
- How will the seller use any cash received?
- Is there really a need for cash or just a "want?"

personal property—All property other than real estate such as cars, boats, furniture, etc.

dead asset—An asset that an investor does not want. In the investor's eyes, it has limited value.

time-share—A form of property ownership under which a property is held by a number of people, each with the right of possession for a specified time interval.

notes:

- Is the seller security conscious?
- Why is the seller offering the property for sale?
- How did the seller arrive at the offering price?
- What is the seller's attitude toward price versus terms (would the seller accept a higher price for the property in return for zero interest)?
- How long has the property been on the market?
- How desperate is the seller to sell the property quickly?
- Is there any evidence of environmental problems, such as lead paint, formaldehyde, or radon gas?

All these things will play into how you approach the seller. For example, if the down payment is going to be used to acquire something or pay a debt, you might be able to acquire the item for him or her and put it on your credit card. Or, you might be able to assume a seller's liability. The seller might be using the cash to take a trip overseas, to purchase furniture, or even buy a new automobile—in which case, you might agree to pay for the trip or furniture, or even lease an automobile for him or her. If the seller has outstanding bills at a department store or to a professional, like a doctor, you might be able to contact the department store or professional and arrange to assume repayment responsibility for the debt, or even obtain a discount by paying the debt in full.

> *"Flexible sellers exist for many reasons—not all of them are down on their luck."*

Be aware that the needs and wants of a seller can change daily. For example, an offer you make today that is rejected by the seller might very well be one that he or she would accept a week or a month from now. Also, if you make an offer that is rejected, there might be another offer you could make that would be equally satisfying to you, and that would be acceptable to the seller.

There is a great tendency, even on the part of experienced investors, to approach a seller with blinders on—which is a bad thing to do. You should never jump to conclusions about the seller's situation. In short, you need to know the seller's situation as thoroughly as possible—to try to get into the seller's mind, prior to making an offer.

Identifying Financing Sources

As I noted previously, as a real estate investor you have a wide array of financing sources available to you. These sources include conventional institutional and private lenders, as well as less traditional sources. Creative sources include things like promissory notes, partners, life insurance policies, and government programs. The more familiar you are with the sources that are available to you, the better able you will be to make knowledgeable and creative decisions when it comes to financing your purchases.

notes:

Conventional Sources

Most people are familiar with the idea that institutional lenders loan money for the purchase of homes. Many people are not aware, however, of the role that private lenders can play in making loans for investment properties.

Institutional Lenders

As I mentioned before, sources that are not traditional can be combined with institutional lender sources, like banks, mortgage companies, and savings and loans, which are what most people consider the primary sources for funding when purchasing a home. As I mentioned in Chapter 5, *Establishing and Improving Your Credit*, it pays to develop a relationship with one or more bankers—if only to keep your options open when it comes to financing. Also, some of the techniques I describe in this chapter for buying real estate with no money down require the buyer to have good credit. In the past few years, the market has forced traditional lenders to create loan products that accommodate 100% financing.

I want to be sure and mention that my website—*www.CarletonSheets.com*—provides instant access to mortgage loan companies. You can apply for a mortgage online and consult with a representative of a company that wants to approve your loan.

In today's mortgage market, there are FHA and Fannie Mae loans that allow borrowers to borrow from 97% to 100% of the purchase price. A list of lenders approved to provide these loan programs is available at *www.hud.gov.* There are also numerous loan programs offered by private lenders that provide 100% financing, and other programs that allow borrowers to combine an 80% first loan with a 20% second loan to accomplish 100% financing. Consulting with a competent mortgage broker, like those available at my website, can provide you with a lot of helpful information on current loan programs.

Private Lenders

If you encounter difficulty obtaining the desired loan terms from an institutional lender, you should seek out a private lender. To do so, check the classified ad section in your local newspaper. You will find that there are private lenders who advertise that they will buy mortgages for cash. As an alternative, you can go to a local mortgage broker or even a real estate broker or agent who represents or knows of private investors. For a resource on note sellers and purchasers, log onto *www.SheetsCoach.com*. This site provides a portal to a service that enables individuals to search for notes to purchase or post notes for sale.

Creative Sources

The underlying idea of this whole course is to be creative when you think about financing your real estate purchases. I can't stress enough how large a factor creativity is in whether or not you succeed as a real estate investor. Some of the

notes:

many possibilities at your disposal when it comes to finding financing include the following 16 sources:

- The seller
- The property
- Promissory notes
- Investors
- Equity partners
- Tenants
- Real estate agents and brokers
- Home equity loans
- Life insurance policies
- Equities in other real and personal properties
- Existing loans on the property
- Using notes
- Pledged-asset mortgages
- Lease options
- Government programs
- Your services and skills

The Seller

The seller can be one of your best sources for creative financing if he or she is willing to participate in the financing of your purchase. Typically, the seller's participation in financing takes the form of a second mortgage—which is an agreement between you and the seller that specifies how much the seller will loan you and how much interest you are to pay, as well as the length of the loan. The second mortgage can be secured by the property itself, other property you already own, or by financial instruments like stocks and bonds.

When the required down payment is only a few thousand dollars or when you are a few thousand dollars short, a flexible seller might agree to a delayed down payment six to 12 months after the *closing date*. Offering the seller a high interest rate can help you achieve this. Many sellers would find an interest rate that is, say, 3% to 6% higher than the current market rate to be very attractive and might even spread the down payment over a long period of time (for example, 24 to 48 months). On a relatively small amount of money, the higher interest rate does not actually cost you that much more and, of course, it is *tax deductible*.

closing date—A predetermined date, agreed to by the buyer and the seller, that the transaction of buying/selling property will take place.

tax deductible—Not subject to taxation. An expense that is deductible from income in determining one's taxable income.

> *"A good source of capital for the beginning investor can be found in the investor's own home or investment property."*

The Property

In some cases, you can use the property itself, even before you own it, to generate funds that can be used for the down payment. (An earlier example, in Chapter 4, *Thinking and Acting Creatively*, showed how one student was able to get a local

notes:

lumber company to advance cash in exchange for an agreement allowing them to cut existing trees after the closing.)

Promissory Notes

Promissory notes are agreements between you and another party whereby the other party agrees to loan money to you in exchange for your promise to pay a specified amount of interest, and to make a specified number of regular payments to pay off the loan. Promissory notes are used when giving the seller a second mortgage on a property. They can also be used with other investors.

Investors

Third-party investors can be useful sources of funds for no down payment investing. Keep in mind that investors usually expect to receive a high rate of return on their investments. Potential investors can be found by searching the financial services section of your local newspaper or in major national newspapers, or on the Internet. The "return" is usually in the form of interest, but it could also be in the form of a percentage of the profit that you will eventually earn on your ownership of the property.

Equity Partners

Equity partners can be invaluable as sources of funds for your real estate investing career. It is possible to make front-end compensation just by putting together the partnership and/or by managing income property purchased by the partnership. For more information about partnerships, see Chapter 21, *Working With Partners*.

Tenants

If you're buying an income property, you can use the credits you receive at closing from the tenants' *security deposits*, last-month's rent, and/or collected rents to reduce or eliminate the down payment the seller requires to sell the property. In some cases, such credits, combined with credits for deferred real estate taxes, can be large enough that you can leave the closing with cash in your pocket. However, I caution you to maintain the appropriate reserves for the payment of taxes and to follow the laws regarding security deposits.

> *security deposit* —An amount of money paid by a tenant before moving into the premises to cover any possible damage incurred while living there, or to protect the landlord in the event that the tenant leaves without being current on rent payments. If the tenant is current and the unit only has a normal amount of wear and tear, then the deposit is generally refunded (also known as an indemnification deposit).

> *"One of the advantages of becoming a licensed broker yourself is that you can, in most cases, share a portion of the commission. That certainly beats borrowing!"*

Real Estate Brokers and Agents

Real estate commissions are generally 5% to 7% of the purchase price of a property (but in some cases, it can be negotiable). If an independent broker both lists and sells the property, he or she receives the entire commission. If another broker or agent is involved, the commission is usually split 50/50 between them.

Borrowing a portion of the commission, or giving the broker or agent a portion of the ownership in lieu of all or part of the commission is sometimes possible, especially when dealing with a listing broker. If the listing broker is also the selling broker, the commission will not be split, and the broker will be in a better position to loan all or part of it to you.

If you find yourself faced with some initial reluctance on the part of the broker or agent to the idea of borrowing the commission, you might try to make the proposition more attractive by offering to give the broker or agent a promissory note for an amount larger than the commission. For example, if the broker or agent's commission is $10,500, you might consider offering a $10,500 note with a high rate of interest. Or, you might offer a note for, say, $13,000 at a market rate of interest. The note could become due and payable in five to seven years. Generating all or part of the down payment in this way is relatively inexpensive. However, don't be bashful about approaching the broker or agent before the note is due and offering to pay it in full in return for a substantial discount.

> *"Many times a broker will surprise you by agreeing to receive commissions over time."*

Before approaching an agent or broker about borrowing a commission, it is important to understand how commission splits are handled in a real estate office. When a seller lists a piece of property with a broker, the broker's compensation is stated in the *listing agreement*. It is usually computed as a percentage of the total selling price. Within a broker's office, salespeople (the agents) have a splitting arrangement with the managing broker. Generally, the splitting arrangement—for example, 50/50 or 60/40—is predicated on the salesperson's annual productivity. While a seller will generally not know about internal splitting arrangements, an informed seller does know that the commission, due to the agent upon the sale of his or her property, is always negotiable at the time the listing agreement is signed.

In some instances, it may be to your advantage to approach the actual broker who has the listing on the property that interests you. If the listing broker knows that they will receive a full commission rather than having to split their commission, they may be more willing to allow you to borrow a portion of the commission.

Students of mine have not only succeeded in persuading the broker or agent to take a note for his or her commission, they have actually borrowed money from the broker or agent. In one case, the agent went into his pocket for $10,000 to make the transaction work. The agent believed in the property and was to receive a $14,000 commission if the sale went through. To make it work, he

listing agreement —A contract between a seller and a real estate broker allowing the broker to find a buyer for the property. The contract will specify, among other things, the arrangement for the payment of the broker's fee if the property sells. The contract is a "best efforts" pledge.

notes:

actually wrote a check to the buyer for $10,000 and, in return, he received a $24,000 note secured by a mortgage on the property.

A new trend seems to be emerging across the country, with real estate brokers actually advertising a 50% commission rebate. One broker in Florida with whom I spoke, said that the concept provides money to the buyer for all or a portion of the down payment, and he acknowledged that business was brisk. While this may be illegal in some states, it would certainly be to your benefit to screen the brokers in your area to see if there are any that are open to this practice. Even if they don't advertise this rebate, you might find brokers who are willing to rebate 50% of the commission to you, especially if they listed the property.

There are advantages to becoming a licensed real estate broker or agent yourself. As a broker or an agent you can receive a share in the real estate commission offered on the sale of the property. This share may be equivalent to 2% to 3.5% of the purchase price. In some instances, you may be able to use the commission as your down payment or waive your share of the commission to motivate the listing broker to present your offer favorably. You may also waive a portion of your commission and apply a portion to the down payment. In any event, the commission can help in the purchase or negotiation of your closing. For more information on the pros and cons of becoming a real estate broker or agent, see Chapter 6, *Setting Up Shop.*

Home Equity Loans

If you already own a home or investment property, that property can serve as a good source of *capital* for you as a beginning investor. Many lending institutions make loans secured by the equity in a home or other property up to 100% or more of the property value. The interest rate for home equity loans is usually tied to the *prime rate,* and it pays to shop for good rates. Some lenders offer a rate as low as the prime rate itself, or even lower. Other lenders might charge as much as 2%, 3%, or even 4% over the prime rate.

Most institutions do not charge any *points (or discounts)* for home equity loans. In addition, the originating costs of the loan are very small and the interest paid may be tax deductible. The typical payoff period for a home equity loan—that is, the time in which the investor is required to repay the loan—is between five and 15 years.

Life Insurance Policies

If you have a whole life insurance policy, you can borrow against its cash value to acquire real estate. The cash values of whole life insurance policies usually earn a low return, and can be an inexpensive way to borrow money to buy real estate.

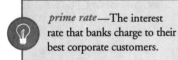
capital—Money used for investing purposes.

prime rate—The interest rate that banks charge to their best corporate customers.

points (or discount) —The percentage of the original balance of the loan that is charged to the borrower by the lender for making the loan. One point equals 1% of the amount of the original balance.

notes:

If you do not have a whole life insurance policy of your own, you might still be able to tap this source of funds by borrowing against someone else's policy. For example, assume that you need a $50,000 down payment to purchase an investment property, and that you have no whole life insurance of your own. To get the money you need, you could contact a local life insurance agent and ask if he or she has a client with a policy that has a cash value of at least $50,000. The policyholder could borrow the $50,000 against his or her policy and loan it to you at perhaps 1% to 2% more interest than he or she pays for the loan. You, in turn, could use this $50,000 as a down payment and perhaps even give the policy owner a 10% to 15% ownership interest in the property as a bonus.

The outstanding loan against a whole life insurance policy reduces the policy payout at time of death. Therefore, if you use this technique, you could take out a term life insurance policy to cover this gap during the payback period. If necessary, you could even take out a term life insurance policy on yourself, naming the owner of the whole life policy that you borrowed against as beneficiary.

This situation represents a truly win/win scenario for all parties. You buy the property you want with no money down (and own an 85% interest in it—if you offered 15% to the policyholder who loaned you the money). If you buy a term policy as suggested, the amount of insurance does not change, and he or she makes a small profit on the interest rate between the policy loan and the loan to you—and also ends up owning 15% of the property.

Before you buy insurance of any kind, make sure you visit my website— *www.CarletonSheets.com.* I have partnered with some outstanding companies that provide quotes on everything from term life insurance to homeowners insurance.

Equities in Other Real or Personal Properties
If you have other real estate or personal properties, whether it is stocks or bonds, a time-share, another income property, a vacant lot, a boat, 10 acres of desert land, or even a diamond ring, you may have some equity in that property. You could use the actual asset as a down payment; you could borrow against the equity; or you might use the property as additional collateral.

Existing Loans on the Property
Many properties have existing assumable loans. If you find a property with an assumable loan, you can assume the loan rather than taking out a new loan on the property.

Using Notes
You can greatly increase your purchase options by using notes. When you create a note, your promise to pay becomes a written and enforceable promise. This promise can be sold, collateralized, pledged, divided, or partially assigned. There

is so much that you can do with notes. They afford buyers numerous alternatives to meet the needs of the seller. Let's look at a few ways notes can be used to meet the needs of the seller and purchase property with little or no down payment:

<u>Sell the Paper at a Discount</u>
There is an active market of investors who are eager to purchase notes at a discount. While this is probably the least desirable way to generate cash, selling a $10,000 note for $7,000 to $7,500 is not difficult, depending upon its interest rate, terms, the creditworthiness of the maker, and the strength of the collateral, if any. This process is known as discounting a note.

One of my students in Chicago used this technique very successfully many years ago. He found a two-bedroom townhouse on the market for $38,000. It had an assumable FHA mortgage with an existing balance of $28,500. The seller wanted $9,500 in cash. My student offered $33,000 for the property and agreed to assume the FHA mortgage of $28,500, but made the contract contingent upon his finding a second mortgage for $4,500.

He then went to the "financial services" section of the classified ads in his local newspaper and started calling people and companies who had advertised in that section. He finally was able to locate a self-employed individual who was acting as trustee for his own pension and profit-sharing trust. After checking my student's credit (it wasn't bad; he just had very little of it), looking at the property, and examining the recent appraisal, he agreed to loan $4,500 cash in return for a $6,000 promissory note and mortgage with interest at 12%. The terms of the note were interest-only for five years with the entire principal balance due at that time. My student was able to buy the property with no money down and, even with the first and second mortgage payments, he still had over a $100 per month positive cash flow.

Investors who make loans like this and who buy discounted notes are always looking at a balance of risk and reward. In this case, the reward was a 22.7% return on the investor's $4,500 investment. You can calculate the return by multiplying five years times the $720 per year interest he was receiving for a total of $3,600, and adding to that the difference between the amount of money that he loaned ($4,500) and the amount of money he was receiving at the end of five years ($6,000), or a difference of $1,500. The total is $5,100 which, when divided by five years, is a $1,020 per year return. This, as a percentage of $4,500, is 22.7%. The downside or risk for the investor was simply having to foreclose on the property that had a $38,000 appraisal, a first mortgage balance of

notes:

approximately $28,000, the $4,500 that he had invested, plus whatever the cost of the foreclosure would be.

This is another example of a win/win situation where the lender was getting an excellent return on his investment with a minimum of risk, the seller was receiving cash at closing, and my student was able to buy a property with no down payment.

Collateralize the Paper

A seller could take a note to a bank, with which the seller has a good banking relationship, and pledge that note as security for borrowing money. While the seller may be paying 3% to 4% more for the money than the amount received from you in interest, this is a negotiable point. You may ultimately have to pay the seller the same interest rate that the seller will have to pay to a bank if he or she collateralizes the note.

A variation of this technique would call for you to create a note and mortgage on property you currently own that has equity. You, in turn, could use that note and mortgage as collateral for money you would borrow either from a bank or a private individual. This could be a relatively inexpensive way to generate cash.

Use the Paper As a Down Payment to Purchase Real Estate

You, the buyer, might give the seller a note for $10,000 secured by a mortgage on the real estate you are purchasing from him or her. The seller could then use the note at its full face value to purchase another property.

Many sellers of property are glad to receive paper that is secured by real estate other than the property they are selling. The seller to whom you are giving the note will find it easier to use that note as a down payment than they might suspect. Once the new property is acquired, the seller could then use any number of ways to take cash out of the equity in the new property.

Sell the Income From the Note

Most people are aware that when they receive a note, they have an asset in the amount of the note. What most people do not realize is that they really have two assets; they have the note itself and also the cash flow that is coming each month or year from that note.

Assume that you gave the seller a $12,000 promissory note bearing interest at 10%, payable $1,200 per year. That $1,200 per year income that the seller is receiving could be sold at a discount or, for that matter, the

notes:

seller could sell several years of income at a discount to generate cash. This technique would leave the primary asset, the $12,000 note, untouched.

The concepts presented above demonstrate a few of the numerous ways notes can be used to help you purchase property with little or no money down. Listen carefully to the seller and use your creativity to develop methods of using notes to complete your own purchases.

Pledged-Asset Mortgages

A pledged-asset mortgage works by using an asset as additional security to induce a lender to make a loan. You use an asset that you own, or that a family member or even a friend owns, as collateral. The lender who accepts the pledged-asset mortgage does not have the right to convert the asset into cash unless you go into default on the loan, and they have to foreclose.

Banks generally will not charge more than current market rates for such loans, which makes them very attractive. The program, as it is currently administered at credit unions or federally insured banks, accepts only certificates of deposit (CDs) as collateral. The CD must account for at least 10% of the price paid for an owner-occupied property or 20% for an investor-owned property. The owner of the CD continues to receive the interest from the CD. Once a payment history is established and the agreed-upon minimum equity position is achieved, the CD is released to the person who pledged it.

I am convinced that some banks would be flexible enough to accept a pledged asset other than a CD from a creditworthy borrower. Why do I say this? Because, more and more, banks are showing some flexibility. As an example of this flexibility, some banks are willing to accept a paydown of interest rates by a seller. For a negotiated amount, a seller could pay for a reduced interest rate on a bank loan for a period of several years that may be as much as 3% or 4% below the current market rate. Some banks will even allow a down payment to be gifted by a seller or a family member of the borrower.

If you do not have any cash for a down payment, be creative in your negotiations with banks in suggesting ways in which they might loan 100% of the purchase price of a property. Remember that while bankers are schooled in the more traditional way of loaning money, if you present some new and creative ways to obtain 100% financing, they might be open to them.

Lease Options

If you don't have money for a down payment on a property, a lease option, or a lease purchase option as they are sometimes referred to, may be just the ticket for you. With a lease option, you, the buyer/lessee, enter into a contract with the seller/lessor, whereby you pay rent and may purchase the property within a speci-

notes:

fied time period. You should insist on having a portion of your rent payment credited toward a predetermined purchase price. A down payment is not required, but the option must be supported by some form of option consideration or nonrefundable deposit. If you ultimately decide not to exercise your option to buy the property, you can potentially sell your option to someone else for cash. In Chapter 12, *Using Lease Options*, I address this topic in great detail.

"The impossible is often the untried."

-Jim Goodwin

Government Programs

Federal, state, and local governments can play a role in your real estate investing. Many cities and towns have real estate related programs that can assist you, and these days all 50 states have housing programs of one kind or another. Every state has a minimum of four housing programs and some, like California and Wisconsin, have up to 25 such programs.

Government housing programs are designed to help people own homes, and many of the programs are geared toward helping specific segments of the population or making certain types of property more attractive to purchase. For example, the Department of Housing and Urban Development (HUD) 203(k) program provides federal loan insurance for loans made by qualified institutions to help families repair or improve, purchase and improve, or refinance and improve existing residential structures that are more than one year old.

FHA and VA underwriting guidelines allow federally sanctioned 501(c)(3) charitable organizations to gift some or all of the down payment. These programs enhance already advantageous FHA and VA insured and/or guaranteed loan products by transforming them from 3% to 5% down payment loan products to no money down purchases. For a list of common government programs related to real estate, see Appendix C, *Government Programs.*

Your Services and Skills

Sometimes, you can use your own services and skills to reduce or eliminate the down payment that would otherwise be required to purchase a property. Also, your sweat equity can pay off handsomely if you decide to buy, rehabilitate, and resell properties.

Developing the Strategy

Once you have assessed the situation and determined which financing source(s) are available to you, it's time to develop a strategy—that is, the exact approach or combination of approaches that you will use to purchase the property. There are many strategies you can use. The following examples, some of which I have already presented, are the most commonly used. Your familiarity with them will greatly improve your ability to purchase properties creatively.

- **Real estate mortgage**—The buyer pledges their interest in the subject property as collateral for a promise to pay an underlying debt. If the buyer defaults on the debt payments, the creditor

notes:

junior mortgage —A mortgage with a secondary interest. A mortgage that is junior to another mortgage lien.

(seller, private investor, or bank) may foreclose on the property. The loan secured by a mortgage can take many forms and can be given by a lending institution, a private investor, or the seller. When the seller provides the loan in exchange for a mortgage and the buyer's promise to make payments, the strategy is sometimes called a seller carry-back or purchase money mortgage (which are explained later).

A given property can serve as collateral for more than one loan; therefore, it is possible to have more than one mortgage on a property. If a property has more than one mortgage, the mortgages become first, second, and so on, based on their order of filing in the public record. In the event of a loan default, the first mortgage has first rights to the property. The second mortgage and all others are said to be *junior mortgages* or subordinate to the first.

• **Seller carry-back**—The seller loans money to the buyer to assist in the purchase of the subject property. The loan is secured by a mortgage on the property being purchased. A seller carry-back loan can occupy any position among the mortgages on the property—that is, first, second, and so on. These mortgages are referred to as purchase money mortgages.

• **A wraparound mortgage**—This is a variation of a seller second mortgage wherein the seller remains obligated to pay the underlying first mortgage and continues to make payments on the first mortgage loan, and the buyer makes payments to the seller on a new mortgage loan that is subordinate to, and wraps around, the first mortgage.

• **Blanket mortgage**—In addition to the property being purchased, the buyer pledges a mortgage on an unrelated piece of real estate and/or personal property in order to provide additional security. A blanket mortgage is a mortgage secured by the pledge of more than one property as collateral.

• **Subordination**—The buyer negotiates the subordination of an existing mortgage to a position behind a new mortgage. Doing so might enable the buyer to obtain the property at a discount or obtain a new first mortgage. For example, let's assume that there's an existing institutional first mortgage on a property you are trying to purchase. The seller has agreed to accept a purchase money second mortgage to assist you in buying his or her property. You purchase the property and then seek to refinance the property by obtaining a new first mortgage. By the seller agreeing to subordinate his/her purchase money second mortgage, it will be possible for you to get a new institutional first mortgage. And after paying off the old first mortgage, it may even be possible to put cash in your pocket.

- **Assumption**—This might represent partial or complete payment of the purchase price. The seller might or might not be released from the obligation to pay on the loan, depending on whether the lender holding the mortgage is willing to accept the buyer in the seller's place. In the case of a qualified assumption, the seller is released from the obligation. In the case of an unqualified assumption, the seller is not released and is still liable.

- **Lease option**—The buyer becomes a tenant in the property and pays rent pursuant to the terms of a lease. A portion of the rent payment will usually go toward the purchase of the property. The buyer also has the right to purchase and resell the property at the end of the lease option period, or sublease it to a tenant in the meantime.

- **Rental participation**—The buyer receives a lower price or other favorable terms in exchange for giving the seller the right to participate in rental income above a predetermined level.

- *Land contract*—The buyer agrees to purchase real estate in installments. The buyer receives an equitable interest in the property and, upon completion of the required payments, the seller deeds the property to the buyer.

- **Outside equity**—The buyer pledges property such as notes, personal or real property as security for the promise to pay the purchase price. The buyer might also transfer, sell, or mortgage some other property to obtain the funds required for a down payment or complete payment on the purchase of a property.

- **Partnership**—Another person or persons aid the buyer in the purchase of real estate. The partners might provide assistance to the buyer in the form of cash to buy the property, or by extending their creditworthiness to help the buyer borrow money in return for an equity ownership. (Also referred to as equity partners.)

land contract—A contract for the sale of real property wherein the seller is obligated to provide a transferable title after the buyer has paid for the property, usually in installments. (Also called an agreement for deed.)

notes:

- **Discounted purchase**—The buyer attempts to purchase real estate as far below market value as possible. Distressed properties are usually good candidates for this technique.

- **Purchase credits**—The buyer negotiates to use security deposits, rent credits, and real estate tax credits to reduce the amount of cash required for the down payment on an income property. This can also cover closing costs, or even provide cash at closing for repairs or reserves, or cash to buyer's pocket.

As I will demonstrate in Chapter 11, *Using Creative Financing Techniques*, you can use these strategies alone or in combination with other strategies to buy property creatively.

REVIEW
Summary

To build true wealth as a real estate investor, you must learn to develop and use creative financing techniques. Determining which creative financing techniques to use is based on a complete knowledge of the situation—from the standpoint of the property, the buyer, and the seller. It also requires knowledge of creative financing sources—like the seller and existing equity in other real or personal property owned by you, or a friend, or a partner.

Every creative financing strategy is unique to its situation, but many share common features. Some common features include persuading the seller to participate in financing your purchase, and the use of promissory notes. Specific features of individual techniques that have worked in the past for my students and me include lease options, blanket mortgages, wraparound mortgages, and land contracts.

Questions

- What are the "Three S's" involved in developing a creative financing technique? (See page 10-2.)

- What three aspects of a purchase must you take into account to completely assess a situation when determining which creative financing technique to use? (See page 10-3.)

- What are three of the creative financing sources available to the real estate investor? (See page 10-6.)

ACTION STEPS

To effectively employ creative financing techniques, you must educate yourself not only on what techniques are available, but also which ones are available to you given your own personal situation (credit, equities, etc.). You should begin compiling information right now that will help you when it comes to developing new techniques.

1. Investigate your current credit situation, including how much money you could borrow, if you had to, from an institutional lender.

2. If you own a home, find out how much money you could borrow against the home in the form of a home equity loan.

3. If you have a whole life insurance policy, find out how much money you could borrow against the policy.

4. Compile a list of at least three people who might be interested in forming a partnership with you for the sake of real estate investing.

5. Familiarize yourself with the *Promissory Note* included in my *Real Estate Forms Portfolio.*

FINAL COMMENTS

The techniques I describe in the next chapter are the result of trial, error, knowledge, market changes, and creative thinking. I venture to say that I'm probably much better equipped than you are, at the moment, to develop creative financing techniques—but that's because I've been doing it for over 30 years! I truly believe, and can't emphasize enough, that if you apply yourself to continuing your education, open your mind to creative thinking, and study the techniques I have described here, you will develop your own legacy as an outstanding (and wealthy) real estate investor!

NOTES

NOTES

INNOVATE

*"People often ask me which **creative real estate technique** I would recommend they use when purchasing property.*

*While I would like to give them a magic answer, the truth is, that the best real estate techniques are the ones **you develop** that work best for you.*

*As a matter of fact, some of my **most profitable transactions** were made possible by combining techniques."*

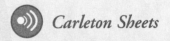 *Carleton Sheets*

11

USING CREATIVE FINANCING TECHNIQUES

As I explained in Chapter 10, *Developing Creative Financing Techniques*, to develop a creative financing technique, you must possess a complete knowledge of the situation—from the standpoint of the property, the buyer, and the seller. You must also be aware of the many creative financing sources that are available to you (like the seller, and existing equity in other property owned by you or a friend, or partner) and the types of strategies you can use to make the transaction work. Many creative financing techniques share common features, including the buyer's ability to persuade the seller to participate in financing the purchase and the use of promissory notes.

In this chapter, you will learn:

- 19 specific creative financing techniques that have been developed from the principles I described in Chapter 10, *Developing Creative Financing Techniques*.

- How to combine various techniques to overcome purchase obstacles.

When you complete this chapter, you will be able to:

- Draw upon your knowledge of specific, fully developed creative financing techniques when considering your options for a no money down real estate transaction.

- Choose the appropriate techniques and technique combinations for some of the most common purchase scenarios.

notes:

FINDING FINANCING METHODS THAT WORK

Over the years, I have used the concepts I described in Chapter 10, *Developing Creative Financing Techniques*, to develop techniques that have proven to be very successful. Although you can develop an unlimited number of techniques with the concepts I have described, I want to present to you 19 proven techniques that I, and/or my students, have used over and over for years.

EXAMPLE TECHNIQUES

The 19 techniques that I have included in this chapter can be grouped into three categories:

- Mortgage and seller financing
- Negotiation and partners
- Land contract and lease option

Table 11.1 summarizes the techniques I describe in this chapter and places them in the appropriate categories:

Table 11.1: Summary of Example Techniques

Type	Number	Description
Mortgage and Seller Financing Techniques	1	Combine New First Mortgage and Seller Second Mortgage
	2	Combine Assumption and Seller Second Mortgage
	3	Combine Assumption, Seller Second Mortgage, and Refinance Loan
	4	Combine Assumption and New Third-Party Second Mortgage
	5	Combine Assumption and Promissory Note
	6	Defer a Portion of the Purchase Price
	7	Combine New First Mortgage and Pledged Asset
	8	Combine New First Mortgage and Bonds
	9	Use Wraparound Mortgage
	10	Use Blanket Mortgage
	11	Combine Assumption and Net Deal

> *"The only thing that overcomes hard luck is hard work."*
> –Harry Golden

notes:

Negotiation and Partner Techniques	12	Negotiate Purchase Credits
	13	Negotiate Position of Private First Mortgage and Use New First Mortgage
	14	Negotiate Discount Purchase and Use New First Mortgage
	15	Negotiate Discount Purchase of Distressed Properties
Land Contract and Lease Option Techniques	16	Use Investors and New First Mortgage
	17	Use Rental Participation
	18	Use Land Contract
	19	Use Lease Option

As you study these techniques, you'll start to get a feel for how you can use the concepts I described in Chapter 10, *Developing Creative Financing Techniques.* Remember to be creative, don't set limits, and don't presume you know what the seller will or will not accept.

Technique 1: Combine New First Mortgage and Seller Second Mortgage

This technique involves combining an institutional or private loan with seller financing to create a no money down purchase strategy. Many institutional lenders have designed programs in which they finance 80% to 95% of the purchase and allow the seller to provide a second mortgage for the balance of the purchase price—resulting in 100% financing. You should also note that many lenders also offer 100% financing, although generally at higher interest rates. If you borrow more than 80% of the value of a property on a first mortgage, you may have to pay the premiums for private mortgage insurance (PMI). This technique is very commonly used, and most mortgage lenders should be able to give you loan program information on this type of loan product. You can also visit *www.CarletonSheets.com.*

Situation, Source(s), and Strategy

Ingredient	Description
Situation	You obtain an institutional or private loan approval for 80% of the proposed purchase price. The loan approval provides that you may borrow the balance from the seller. You negotiate a purchase whereby the seller will provide the balance of the financing.
Source(s)	• An institutional or private lender • The seller

notes:

Strategy   Take out a new first mortgage on the property and obtain
financing from the seller to cover the balance of the
purchase price.

Example
The seller of a home valued at $150,000 has an existing loan of $80,000 and is
looking for a full-price offer, but is willing to accept $30,000 of the full price
over 10 years at 5% interest. To use this technique, you would:

1. Obtain a new first mortgage for $120,000 or 80% of the purchase price
   and appraised value—the loan amount would pay off the seller's $80,000
   mortgage and provide the seller with $40,000 cash at closing less any clos-
   ing expenses or charges.

2. Give the seller a second mortgage in the amount of $30,000. Now, in
   addition to the funds received at closing, the seller has a note and mortgage secured by the property that will be paid in full in 10 years. The seller
   has been able to get the full asking price, and you have bought a property
   with no money down.

Comments
If you encounter difficulty obtaining the new first mortgage, you may look to
the seller. Some sellers have been known to join the buyer in signing a note and
mortgage. If the buyer does not have sufficient credit to get a new mortgage, the
seller, in effect, loans his or her credit to the buyer. The property is then transferred after the new loan is in place. You could even use the credit of an equity
partner to secure the financing, in return for which the partner would receive a
percentage of ownership.

Technique 2: Combine Assumption and Seller Second Mortgage
This technique involves assuming an existing loan on the property and taking
out a second loan with the seller for the balance. When you assume a mortgage,
you take on the seller's obligation to pay. Accordingly, you must be certain to
understand the terms of the mortgage and note you are assuming. The interest
rate, outstanding balance, and loan terms are major factors in determining your
cash flow or resale profit. When you assume a loan, you inherit the seller's loan
terms—be they good or bad. Obviously this technique works best when the seller's mortgage has a desirable fixed interest rate with no impending rate increase
or **balloon payment** due.

The seller may or may not be released from the responsibility of paying on the
loan—depending on whether your assumption is qualified or unqualified. If your
assumption is qualified, the lender will likely review your credit and income. If the
lender does not qualify you to replace the seller, you may still be able to assume

> *balloon payment* —A large
> final payment due on a
> note, usually after partial
> amortization of the debt
> through installment payments.

notes:

the loan. However, the lender will not release the seller from the responsibility to pay on the debt. In other words, if you default, the lender will seek to recover from both you and the seller. In any case, with an assumption, you avoid many of the loan costs customarily charged when you create a new loan.

The second component of this technique involves obtaining seller financing for the balance of the purchase price. The two mortgages you create cover the entire purchase price. You may offer a seller the upper end of the property's value to encourage flexibility.

Situation, Source(s), and Strategy

Ingredient	Description
Situation	You want to buy a property that has an assumable mortgage without using a down payment. The seller is flexible and willing to take a second mortgage on the property.
Source(s)	• An institutional or private lender • The seller
Strategy	Assume the seller's first mortgage, and give the seller a second mortgage for the balance of the purchase price (seller's equity).

Example

You find a home on the market for $150,000 that has an existing assumable mortgage of $75,000. The seller is willing to finance a portion of the purchase price. The seller is more concerned with getting his or her full asking price rather than receiving cash at closing. To use this technique, you would:

1. Assume the $75,000 mortgage on the property.

2. Offer the seller a second mortgage for the balance of the purchase price ($75,000).

In this case you end up with two mortgages—the assumed first mortgage and the second mortgage given to the seller—but you have purchased the property with no money down.

Comments

This technique is a very efficient and cost-saving method of acquiring property. Lenders are usually capable of processing assumed mortgages quicker than they can process and fund new loans. Therefore, you can probably close quicker and at a lower cost with this method.

Note that this technique works best when the seller does not need cash at closing. However, the seller can still receive cash at closing, or at a time after closing, by selling all or part of his second mortgage for a discount to an investor.

Technique 3: Combine Assumption, Seller Second Mortgage, and Refinance Loan

This technique involves assuming the loan on a mortgaged property, obtaining seller financing by offering an attractive rate of return, and refinancing at a later time (perhaps right away) at a more desirable rate. This technique resolves two common obstacles faced by no money down buyers. One common obstacle is obtaining a purchase loan without a down payment. The requirements for obtaining a refinance loan differ from a purchase loan. The amount loaned to refinance is based on the property's appraised value. This amount may be substantially larger than the initial purchase price, thus allowing the borrower to obtain a higher loan amount with a refinance loan than with a purchase loan. As long as the amount loaned covers the existing liens, the borrower does not have to bring money to closing—and may actually take cash out at closing. Although there are some refinance loan programs that don't require the borrower to have owned the property for a specified period of time (this is known as a *seasoning* requirement), many programs require the borrower to have owned the property for at least a year.

Armed with the knowledge that you will be able to quickly refinance the property, you can be more aggressive in your negotiations with the seller. You may be able to overcome the seller's objection to provide financing by offering premium interest rates.

seasoning—As used in the mortgage industry; the requirement of ownership for a specified period of time.

Situation, Source(s), and Strategy

Ingredient	Description
Situation	The seller does not require cash at closing and is willing to wait for the portion of the purchase price not assumed, provided a premium rate of interest is paid.
Source(s)	• An institutional or private lender • The seller
Strategy	Have a mortgage broker verify how long you must own the property before you will be eligible for a refinance loan. Ask the seller to assist in financing your purchase, and offer a premium rate of interest on the loan. Structure the agreement so that the term of the seller's loan (second mortgage) is of medium range—for example, five years. At the end of the loan

notes:

term, or most likely even sooner, refinance the debt using your equity in the property and use the new loan to pay off the second mortgage.

Example

A seller has a property and, because he needs a quick sale, is willing to accept $150,000 for it. The property has an appraised value of $175,000 and, with some relatively minor improvements, you believe it could be appraised for $200,000. It also has an existing assumable mortgage of $80,000 payable at the rate of $644 per month. The seller wants $20,000 cash at closing and is willing to extend a loan of $50,000 to you in the form of a mortgage at 10% interest. You have no cash for a down payment and need the seller to loan you the difference between the asking price ($150,000) and the amount of the assumable loan ($80,000). To use this technique, you would:

1. Agree to assume the existing $80,000 mortgage, and offer to pay the seller 15% interest for a period of five years on a second mortgage for the remaining $70,000. This way the seller is receiving a premium rate of interest for accepting a note instead of cash.

2. At or before the end of the five-year loan term, refinance the entire debt—that is, what remains of the $80,000 assumed mortgage plus what you owe the seller for the second mortgage. If you are capable of refinancing sooner and paying the seller off, you may be able to negotiate a lower principal balance. You might propose that the seller accept less than the outstanding balance if you pay it off within 15 months.

Under this arrangement, the seller receives a monthly payment of $875 ($70,000 times 15%, divided by 12 months) for five years, all of which is interest paid on the second mortgage. Your total monthly payment for those five years is $1,519 ($644 in payment on the assumed loan plus $875 in interest to the seller). At or before the end of the loan term, you will refinance and obtain a new first mortgage that will pay off the first and second mortgage. You may be able to negotiate a reduction in the mortgage balance in exchange for an early payoff.

Comments

If your total monthly payment of $1,519 will result in a negative cash flow, and you still want to offer 15% interest, you can restructure the second mortgage so that only a portion of the 15% interest is paid monthly. If you do so, you should make sure that the interest accumulates but does not compound—so that, at the end of five years, you owe the original $80,000 plus the deferred interest—but not interest on the interest. Begin now to shop for refinancing alternatives with local mortgage brokers.

Technique 4: Combine Assumption and New Third-Party Second Mortgage

This technique involves combining an assumption with a third-party second mortgage. It relies on the willingness of the seller to accept an offer that is contingent on your ability to assume the existing loan and obtain a second mortgage on the property.

Situation, Source(s), and Strategy

Ingredient	Description
Situation	You are approved for a second mortgage. In other words, a lender is willing to provide financing to assist in your purchase knowing that the lien will be in a position inferior to another mortgage. The seller has an assumable loan and wants a cash down payment. He or she is willing to accept an offer that is contingent on your ability to obtain a new (third-party) second mortgage on the property to generate the down payment.
Source(s)	• Institutional or private lender
Strategy	Offer to assume the property's existing first mortgage and pay the balance of the purchase price with the proceeds from a new second mortgage. The contract should be written contingent on your ability to obtain a second mortgage to cover the balance due after your assumption of the first mortgage.

Example

You have found a property on the market for $150,000 that has an existing $125,000 assumable mortgage. The seller has $25,000 equity ($150,000 minus $125,000) and wants to receive it all in cash. The property has been on the market for five months without selling, and the owner is getting anxious. To use this technique, you would:

1. Offer the seller $145,000 contingent upon being able to locate a new second mortgage.

2. Find a lender to loan you $20,000 in the form of a second mortgage on the property.

3. Assume the $125,000 first mortgage.

By offering to give the seller $20,000 in cash and assume the $125,000 first mortgage, you are proposing to pay $145,000 for the property ($125,000

notes:

assumed mortgage plus $20,000 cash). This is not a bad offer for the property considering that it has been on the market for five months.

Comments

Banks are generally reluctant to make second mortgage loans in situations like this, because the property is already subject to an existing loan for a little more than 80% of its fair market value. Therefore, it will probably be necessary to go to a private lender or mortgage broker for the second mortgage. There are some lenders that will extend a home equity line of credit. You may also find ads for private lenders in the classified ad section in your local newspaper. Many of them advertise that they are willing to buy mortgages for cash. When you locate a lender, tell them the appraised value of the property, the size of the existing first mortgage, and the amount of cash that you need. When you find out how much they are willing to lend you, and the interest rate on the loan, perform a financial analysis of the property to determine whether or not the net operating income will support the combined payments of the first and second mortgages.

Technique 5: Combine Assumption and Promissory Note

This technique enables you to accommodate a seller who requires cash at a no down payment closing. In addition to assuming any existing mortgage, this technique involves creating a promissory note and finding someone to purchase it. Promissory notes can be sold, discounted, or exchanged. Every note has a *face value* and, in some cases, is secured by some form of collateral.

> *face value* —In reference to a note, the face value is the full amount for which the note has been written.

Discounting a promissory note means selling the note for less than its face value. When you sell a note at a discount, the purchaser of the note usually buys the rights to all future payments generated by the note—both in interest paid on the note and any balance due at the end of the term. There is an active market of investors who are eager to purchase notes at a discount. Your ability to sell a note will depend on the interest rate and terms of the note, your creditworthiness as the note maker, and the strength of the collateral, if any, associated with the note.

Situation, Source(s), and Strategy

Ingredient	Description
Situation	You want to purchase a property with an assumable FHA mortgage and provide cash to the seller at closing without putting any money down.
Source	• Institutional lender • Note buyer
Strategy	Offer to assume the existing mortgage and create a note. Locate a note purchaser to purchase the note at closing.

Example

You find a condominium on the market for $70,000 with an assumable FHA mortgage balance of $60,000. The property appraises for $75,000. The seller is willing to allow the assumption of the first mortgage, but wants $10,000 at closing. To use this technique, you would:

1. Offer to assume the first mortgage.

2. Find an investor who agrees to pay $10,000 in cash in return for a promissory note, with a face value of $15,000 at 12% interest, and secured by a second mortgage on the property being purchased.

This is an example of a win/win situation where the note purchaser gets an excellent return on his investment with a minimum of risk, the seller receives the cash he needs, and the buyer is able to buy the property without using any of his own cash. However, you should only enter into a transaction, with terms like this, if the rental income can cover all of the expenses (including the two mortgage payments) and still leave you with a positive cash flow.

Comments

Notes can be very useful assets in your investing. You can creatively use them in place of cash or as collateral to obtain cash. You can divide them and even sell the income they produce for a specified period of time, while retaining ownership of the principal debt and income balance. In your investing, you should try to recognize creative ways to create, restructure, and sell notes to meet your investment goals.

Technique 6: Defer a Portion of the Purchase Price

In some areas of the country, local real estate prices are such that it is nearly impossible to achieve a break-even or positive cash flow given prevailing market rental rates. This problem can be overcome either by negotiating no-interest or low-interest financing by the seller or by deferring a portion of the purchase price. The latter alternative is usually easier to negotiate and works equally well.

Situation, Source(s), and Strategy

Ingredient	Description
Situation	You want to buy an income property, but prevailing market rental rates make the property not economical unless you can reduce the amount of your monthly payment.
Source(s)	• The seller
Strategy	Persuade the seller to finance your purchase at low or no interest or defer a portion of the purchase price.

notes:

Example

A seller has a three-bedroom, two-bath home on the market for $150,000. The property has an existing $105,000 assumable first mortgage. In return for obtaining his or her full asking price, the seller is willing to take back a mortgage for the balance at the going market rate of interest. The fair market rental rate on the property is $1,500 per month. To use this technique, you would:

1. Offer to assume the first mortgage.

2. Give the seller a second mortgage with two notes totaling $45,000 ($150,000 minus $105,000)—one note for $20,000 at the market rate of interest, and a second for $25,000, also at a market rate of interest, but with the interest deferred for six years.

At the end of six years, you could refinance the loan by paying off the first mortgage plus both notes or, preferably, paying off only the second note for $25,000 plus interest. Ideally, the seller's first note for $20,000 (which was a second mortgage) and the new first mortgage would stay on the property. If the second mortgage is to stay on the property after refinancing, the mortgage would have to include a subordination clause that would be inserted at the time you buy the property and sign the mortgage. (For a description of subordination, see the glossary.)

Comments

When you use a technique like this, you must pay special attention to the type of interest specified in the promissory note—especially that of the note for which you are deferring interest. In particular, you should specify that you will pay simple, rather than compounded interest. For example, if the interest on the $25,000 note is computed as simple interest, you will owe $12,000 in deferred interest in six years. On the other hand, if the interest is specified as compound interest, you will owe $16,300 in deferred interest.

Technique 7: Combine New First Mortgage and Pledged Asset

In this technique, assume you have equity in some real or personal property—for example, stocks, bonds, or other securities, a home, boat, investment property, automobile, or vacant land. You can use these assets as collateral for a mortgage that you would offer the seller. This technique is a good alternative to the New First Mortgage and Seller Second Mortgage Technique (See Technique 1). Under this technique the seller is given an asset as collateral, in addition to the property being sold. You also establish credibility by demonstrating you have assets. You may encourage the seller's acceptance by pledging an asset that is free from any liens, and putting the seller in first position to be paid out in the case of default. Make certain to include a *substitution of collateral clause* in the mortgage.

substitution of collateral clause —A clause in a mortgage that permits the mortgagor (borrower) to substitute property of equal or greater value for the property originally pledged as collateral.

Situation, Source(s), and Strategy

Ingredient	Description
Situation	You want to buy a property with no money down and you have existing equity in assets, such as stocks and bonds, a home, automobile, and/or vacant land. The seller is willing to take a promissory note and a mortgage on the equity in your existing assets in lieu of a cash down payment on the property you want to buy.
Source(s)	• Equity in personal and real estate assets • The seller • An institutional or private lender (as necessary)
Strategy	Give the seller a promissory note in lieu of cash for the down payment on the property you want to buy, and secure the note with a mortgage on the assets. Use seller financing or a mortgage from an institutional or private lender to pay the balance of the price of the property.

Example

You want to buy a two-unit property that is on the market for $200,000 and on which there currently exists an $87,000 mortgage. The seller's equity is $113,000 ($200,000 minus $87,000). To use this technique, you would:

1. Create a promissory note and mortgage in the amount of $40,000 secured by the equity in property that you own—for example, another piece of real estate you own.

2. Offer the $40,000 note to the seller as a down payment on the two-unit property.

3. Obtain a $160,000 first mortgage on the property from an institutional or private lender.

The combination of your promissory note ($40,000) and first mortgage ($160,000) gives the seller the full $200,000 asking price. (As an alternative, you could try to get the seller to take your $40,000 note and a $160,000 wraparound mortgage. For a description of wraparound mortgages, see the glossary.)

When you buy this property, you will immediately have $40,000 equity in the property due to the $40,000 mortgage that is secured by the existing assets that you used as a down payment. If the seller of the two-unit property is concerned about not receiving any cash at the closing, you can show him or her how to convert the

notes:

note and mortgage into cash by selling it to someone else. You may also try to sell the note yourself or obtain a secured loan, or use a credit card for a down payment.

Comments

The mortgage that you create using your existing assets should include a substitution of collateral clause, which allows you to later move the mortgage to another property where you have equivalent or greater equity. For example, you might use the equity in your own home to buy a two-unit property; your equity in the two-unit property to buy a four-unit property; and your equity in the four-unit property to buy an apartment building. The substitution of collateral clause would allow you to move the mortgage from your own personal residence to your most recent purchase—the apartment building.

Technique 8: Combine New First Mortgage and Bonds

This technique makes use of the fact that many flexible sellers would rather receive high quality bonds, instead of real estate, as collateral for a promissory note. A bond is an interest bearing, or non-interest bearing certificate issued by a business or government that promises to pay the holder a specified amount on a specified date. The technique works best when you have a relatively low mortgage in relation to the property's value.

When you buy a bond, you're buying a financial instrument that is structured to possess a certain value at a specified date in the future. For example, if you buy a $1,000 bond that matures 10 years from the date of purchase, you're guaranteed by whomever issued the bond that it will be worth $1,000 in 10 years. The amount you pay for the $1,000 bond depends on the interest rates in effect at the time of purchase, the creditworthiness of the issuer, and the age of the bond, but might typically be between $500 and $700, especially if it's a zero interest bond.

Bonds come in many different forms, including corporate bonds, U.S. government bonds, and tax-free bonds. You'll find listings of private corporate bonds (also known as New York Exchange Bonds) and U.S. government bonds in the daily edition of the *Wall Street Journal*. For tax-free bonds you'll need to contact a stockbroker. In searching for a bond, you should try to find a good, tax-free, zero-interest bond like a city, state, or county revenue bond that will be due in nine or 10 years. Since such bonds are tax-free, there is no tax liability for either the seller or for you.

Situation, Source(s), and Strategy

Ingredient	Description
Situation	You want to buy a property that has a relatively low ratio of mortgage to property value, and you have equity in another property or have a partner who has equity in a property.

notes:

Source(s)   • Bonds

Strategy   Obtain a new first mortgage, and use the funds to pay off the existing first mortgage and provide the seller with some cash. Then give the seller the bonds for the remaining amount due.

Example

A seller has a four-unit property on the market for $400,000. The existing assumable mortgage on the property is $95,000, so the seller has $305,000 in equity. The seller wants at least $100,000 in cash at closing and is willing to finance the balance if given sufficient security. To use this technique, you would:

1. Persuade the seller to accept good quality bonds with a 10-year maturity as collateral for a note.

2. Offer to buy the property with $100,000 cash, due in 90 days; assume the existing $95,000 mortgage; and provide the seller with a note secured by bonds worth $205,000 when they mature.

3. Persuade the seller to deed the property to you with the $305,000 equity and secure the $205,000 you owe to the seller with equity in another property—or perhaps property belonging to a friend or partner.

4. Once you become the owner of the property, obtain a new $340,000 first mortgage. Use the proceeds from the mortgage as follows—$95,000 to pay off the first mortgage, $140,000 (approximately) to buy the $205,000 worth of bonds with a 10-year maturity, $100,000 to pay the seller, and $5,000 cash for yourself. (The amount of cash you'll have will depend on the actual cost of the bonds, as well as closing costs for the new mortgage.)

As a result of this series of transactions, the seller receives $100,000 in cash and owns a $205,000 note secured by bonds that will be worth $205,000 when they mature in 10 years. You now own a $400,000 property with a $340,000 mortgage and have $60,000 in equity. In addition, you have put approximately $5,000 in your pocket.

Comments

This is one of my favorite creative financing techniques because it is simple (despite its apparent complexity) and powerful. However, it is not without potential problems. The problems are these:

1. Under current tax law, if the bonds are taxable, the owner of the bonds will be required to declare interest on the bonds as they increase in value.

notes:

To avoid the yearly declaration of interest, you can use zero-coupon municipal bonds such as those used in the example I just described.

2. Unless the seller is willing to accept no interest on the promissory note, you will have to make interest payments on the note to the seller each year until the bonds mature. This does not have to present a problem, however, as long as you budget properly for the interest you must pay. Don't forget—you will receive cash at the closing.

Keep in mind that this technique is not an attempt to deal in an underhanded way or to fool the seller. Everything should be spelled out and completely understandable to him or her. While the bonds are only worth approximately $140,000 today, they will be worth $205,000 in 10 years. The seller's only risk is loss of the interest you have agreed to pay in the meantime. To overcome this potential risk, you might agree to secure the interest payments with a mortgage on another property you own. Alternatively, if you have the cash on hand, you could even prepay several years' worth of interest or buy a second zero-interest bond for the amount of the interest you'll owe—which could then be used as security for the interest you have agreed to pay. Finally, you might be able to negotiate a zero-interest loan so that you will have no interest payment obligations at all. As in all things related to real estate investing, it pays to be creative and to negotiate.

Technique 9: Use Wraparound Mortgage

When you use a wraparound mortgage, you give a promissory note and second mortgage on the property to the seller—in lieu of cash. The seller retains and continues to pay the underlying first mortgage on the property—which is usually much less than the new second mortgage—and uses the payments received from you on the second mortgage to make the ongoing payments on the first mortgage. When the underlying first mortgage is paid off, the second mortgage automatically moves to first position.

Situation, Source(s), and Strategy

Ingredient	Description
Situation	You want to buy the property without a cash down payment. The seller is willing to take a promissory note and mortgage from you for the entire purchase price while retaining his or her underlying first mortgage on the property.
Source(s)	• The seller
Strategy	Give the seller a note and second mortgage for the entire purchase price of the property.

Example

The seller of a property currently valued at $150,000 acquired the property 14 years ago for $70,000. To buy the property, he made a cash down payment of $5,000 and financed the remaining $65,000 over 25 years at 8.5% interest. As a result, his (assumable) mortgage loan on the property calls for 300 monthly payments of $524, including principal and interest. To date he has made 168 payments and currently owes $44,793 on the original $65,000 loan; therefore, his current equity is $105,207 ($150,000 minus $44,793). To use this technique, you would:

1. Offer the seller a note for $150,000 that's secured by a second wraparound mortgage on the property. The note would be paid off over 25 years at 8.5% interest—which works out to 300 monthly payments at $1,208 each, including principal and interest.

2. Obligate the seller to continue making his own monthly payments on the underlying first mortgage using your payments to him to do so.

The difference between your monthly payment to the seller ($1,208) and the seller's monthly payment on the first mortgage ($524) results in a $684 monthly cash flow for the seller.

Eleven years from the date you purchase the property, the seller will pay off the underlying first mortgage, and you will have paid off $31,650 of your second wraparound mortgage to the seller. The remaining balance of your wraparound mortgage will be $118,350 ($150,000 minus $31,650), which means that the seller's equity will have grown from $105,207 to $118,350 in 11 years—which is a 12.5% increase. And, all the while, the seller was enjoying an annual cash flow of $8,208 (12 times $684).

Comments

This technique allows you to buy a property with no money down without incurring the cost and liability associated with assuming a first mortgage from an institutional or private lender. However, be sure to establish your right to know if the first mortgage is being paid. You can accomplish this by either having an escrow agent collect and disperse funds or break your monthly payments into two payments; one to the seller, and one to the first mortgagee.

Technique 10: Use Blanket Mortgage

A blanket mortgage includes collateral in addition to the property being purchased. For example, you can include equity in your home, another investment property, or even your automobile, as part of a blanket mortgage. Blanket mortgages come in handy when you encounter a seller willing to finance the entire purchase—if given assurance that you will not default on the loan. The seller

notes:

may be afraid that the property will be returned to him or her in worse condition than when it was sold, and that he or she will have to go to the trouble and expense of selling the property all over again. By including equity in property you already own as part of the mortgage on the seller's property, you increase your stake in the property, and assume a greater part of the risk of defaulting on the loan.

Situation, Source(s), and Strategy

Ingredient	Description
Situation	You want to buy a property with no money down. The seller is willing to finance the entire price of the property but is afraid that you will walk away from the loan before you've built up substantial equity in the property.
Source(s)	• Equity in your existing assets • The seller
Strategy	Give the seller a note for the entire purchase price of the property—using the property you are buying as collateral, as well as the equity in other property that you own.

Example

You locate a house in your neighborhood that has been vacant for some time and needs exterior painting. You research the property and get the name and number of the owner, and find out that there is no mortgage on the property.

When you contact the owner you learn that it's a senior who is interested in selling, but has not listed the property with a real estate broker yet. You schedule an interior inspection and determine that the property requires only cosmetic repairs and is habitable in its current condition. Your market analysis reveals the property is worth $90,000.

You determine through conversation with the seller that the property is clearly a burden for him. He tells you that he is a retired teacher and is looking to move closer to family out-of-state. You take into consideration the rent you will be able to charge for the unit, as well as the repairs you would like to make, and negotiate a purchase price of $73,000. You offer to pay the purchase price in the form of a *purchase money mortgage* (seller carry-back).

The seller raises concerns about what will happen if you do not pay on the mortgage or maintain the property. He wishes to retire and move away, and is fearful of the possibility of having to foreclose on the property, or take it back once the transaction closes. To use this technique, you would:

purchase money mortgage —A mortgage given to the seller as part or all of the consideration for the purchase of property. In effect, it is money loaned by the seller to the purchaser.

1. Explain to the seller that you will make the mortgage payments to him on time.

2. If you have a current mortgage on a piece of property and have paid on the mortgage over a long period of time, you could provide the seller with a copy of your mortgage history, which you can order from your lender. This history will show the amount and timeliness of your payments.

3. Present the seller with a blanket mortgage on the seller's property, as well as another piece of property that you own, which has $30,000 in equity. The seller now has the option to foreclose, not only on the property being purchased, but on your mortgaged property as well—should you default.

Comments

You have purchased a property with no money down, and the seller has confidently extended financing to you because of the additional property you mortgaged as security.

This is a good technique for low-priced properties. You should avoid pledging your personal residence unless you are capable of paying the mortgage on the property being purchased in the event of a vacancy. If you do use your personal residence, remember to put a release clause in the mortgage that will allow you to release your personal residence out from under the blanket mortgage after several years of timely payments, or by the payment of a small lump sum amount, for example, $5,000.

Technique 11: Combine Assumption and Net Deal

In a net deal the seller gets a net amount of cash for the property. When a seller's equity in a property is very small, this approach to purchasing the property is extremely effective. All of the costs of closing are paid by the buyer, including transfer taxes, recording fees, title insurance, real estate brokerage commissions, home inspections, and in some cases, even the taxes for the year. The seller knows that whatever amount of money (or notes) that you offer, over and above any debt on the property, is the amount the seller will have at the closing.

This method of buying real estate has several advantages. First, if there is a brokerage commission, it is calculated on a smaller selling price so there are some savings. Second, if the broker is willing to take the commission in the form of a note, the actual cash required can be minimal.

notes:

Situation, Source(s), and Strategy

Ingredient	Description
Situation	You want to buy a property in which the seller has little equity. You're willing to pay closing costs.
Source(s)	• Any
Strategy	Propose to the seller that you pay for closing costs in exchange for consideration on the size of the required down payment.

Example

A seller has a property on the market listed with a broker for $160,000. The listing shows an assumable mortgage of $140,000. The seller wants $6,000 to use as a down payment on a home in another state. To use this technique, you would:

1. Offer the seller $4,000 net for the property and agree to assume the debt.

2. Agree to pay the real estate commission in the form of a note in the amount of $8,640 ($144,000 times 6%) and to pay all transfer taxes, title insurance, and recording fees—expenses that you estimate will cost $1,400.

Thus, your total purchase price will be $154,040 ($140,000 mortgage plus a broker's commission of $8,640, plus $4,000 cash to the seller, plus $1,400 in closing costs), and your cash out-of-pocket will be $5,400 ($4,000 cash to the seller plus $1,400 in closing costs).

Comments

In all the techniques presented, it is useful to determine what the seller wants to net from the transaction. This is, in essence, what they are really trying to accomplish. It will also serve as a helpful negotiation tool—if you meet resistance, you can show the seller how you have devised a solution that nets the desired result.

Technique 12: Negotiate Purchase Credits

This technique employs the use of security deposits, rent credits, and real estate tax credits to reduce the amount of cash required for the down payment on an income property. Sometimes, such credits are substantial enough to allow you to end up taking out cash at closing.

When a tenant signs a lease, he or she is almost always required to put down a security deposit against any damage that might be incurred by the property during the term of the lease. In addition, some landlords (like me) collect the final month's rent at the lease signing. Such security deposits and final-month rents must be turned over to the buyer at closing. Also, the buyer receives credit for part of the rent collected in the current month. For example, if you close on an income property on the 10th day of a month, you will receive credit for approximately two-thirds of the month's rent. If you close on the first day of the month, you will either receive the rents already collected by the seller or will immediately collect the rents yourself.

In addition to security deposits and rent credits at closing, you will also receive a credit for unpaid real estate taxes. Real estate taxes are generally paid in arrears, which means that the seller is always behind in paying taxes. For example, real estate taxes for the current year are due and payable late in the year, or sometime next year. Thus, the buyer receives a credit for the real estate taxes that have accrued but have not been billed prior to closing.

The credits from security deposits, last-month rents, collected rents, and unpaid real estate taxes can all be used to reduce the amount of cash required for the down payment, and sometimes these credits are substantial. On a 10-unit building, for example, there might be $7,000 in security deposits (10 times $700), last-month rents of 10 times the monthly rental rate, and an additional credit for unpaid real estate taxes of $10,000 to $15,000. In such circumstances, it would not be unusual for credits on a 10-unit building to exceed $20,000.

Situation, Source(s), and Strategy

Ingredient	Description
Situation	You are purchasing an income property and want to pay little or no money down on the property.
Source(s)	• Tenant security deposits, last-month rents, collected rents, and unpaid real estate taxes.
Strategy	Use the credits that are due to you as the buyer to reduce the amount of your down payment on the property.

Example

You are purchasing a 10-unit building, each unit of which rents for $600 per month. At closing, on the first day of the month, you are to immediately receive collected rents in the amount of $6,000 (10 times $600), a credit for security deposits of $7,000 (10 times $700), and a credit for the last-month rents of $6,000 (10 times $600). Real estate taxes on the property are $10,000 per year, and at closing you are to receive a real estate tax credit of $8,000. As a result, at

notes:

closing you receive $27,000 in funds and credits (the sum of $6,000 for next month's rent, $7,000 for a security deposit, $6,000 for last-month rents, and $8,000 for real estate taxes not yet billed). To use this technique, you would:

1. Use the $27,000 in credits due at closing to pay or reduce the required down payment on the property or, if possible, to allow you to take out cash at closing.

If you are obtaining a new mortgage on the property, you can use the rents you collect at the end of your first month of ownership to pay your first mortgage payment—which will not be due until the first day of the following month, when you will be receiving another month's rent. If you are assuming an existing mortgage for which the payment is due mid-month, you can talk to the lender about moving the mortgage payment ahead to the first day of the following month. You will probably be required to pay one-half month's interest on the mortgage, but you will benefit by receiving as much as one-half month's rent payments. This extra cash can be used for a down payment on another property, for fixing up the income property, or for your own personal use.

Comments

Keep in mind that, when you buy an income property, you will incur little or no expenses during the first month because mortgage payments and other expenses like utilities are paid in arrears (after you use the service). Since rents are paid in advance, however, you will have one month's worth of rent available to use for purposes other than paying the bills.

Technique 13: Negotiate Position of Private First Mortgage and Use New First Mortgage

In this technique, you get the holder of a private mortgage on a property you want to buy to move his or her mortgage from a senior (first) mortgage position to a junior (second) mortgage position. This enables you to obtain a new first mortgage to buy the property. The technique works well when the private mortgage holder is not willing to *discount* the mortgage in return for a complete payoff.

Situation, Source(s), and Strategy

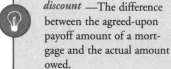

discount —The difference between the agreed-upon payoff amount of a mortgage and the actual amount owed.

Ingredient	Description
Situation	You want to buy a property with no money down. A senior mortgage holder is willing to move the mortgage from a senior to a junior position in exchange for a partial payoff of the loan amount.

Source(s)	• Institutional and/or private lender
Strategy	Offer to pay off part of the private mortgage in exchange for getting it moved from the senior to a junior position. Obtain a new first (senior) mortgage on the property. Use the funds to pay the private mortgage holder the agreed-upon payment, and to pay the seller for his or her equity in the property.

Example

A seller has a property on the market for $150,000. There is an existing private first mortgage on the property in the amount of $75,000. To use this technique, you would:

1. Ask the private mortgage holder to move his or her mortgage from a first (senior) position to a second (junior) position in return for a payment of, say, $25,000 in cash. This $25,000 payment reduces the private mortgage from $75,000 to $50,000. Agree to make the $25,000 payment only after a new first mortgage is secured.

2. Put a new $100,000 first mortgage on the property.

3. Use $25,000 of the money received from the new first mortgage ($100,000) to pay the private mortgage holder for moving the mortgage position. After you make the payment, you will still owe the private mortgage holder $50,000—now in the form of a second mortgage.

4. Pay the remaining $75,000 of the new first-mortgage money to the seller to purchase the property.

This transaction results in the purchase of a $150,000 property with no down payment. You assume a $50,000 loan ($75,000 less the $25,000 pay down to the mortgage holder) and move it to a second position. Then you obtain a loan for the $100,000 balance of the purchase price. You use this loan to pay the seller $75,000 and the private mortgage holder $25,000 (the lump sum payment convinces him to move the private mortgage to a second position). This is also a win/win situation, because the seller gets the full asking price—while you successfully arrange 100% financing ($100,000 first mortgage and $50,000 assumed private mortgage equals $150,000 purchase price).

Comments

If you own property that has a private first mortgage, you can use this same technique to remove your equity for other investment purposes. You should never assume that the private lender would not renegotiate the terms of a mortgage. Under the right circumstances, the private lender may reduce the principal due, the interest rate, or extend the term of the loan.

notes:

When dealing with foreclosure properties, it is often possible to negotiate a reduction of the principal balance of the loan (also known as a short payoff request). You may be able to obtain a property at or below market price, and the foreclosing lender avoids the additional cost and time expended in a complete foreclosure proceeding.

Technique 14: Negotiate Discount Purchase and Use New First Mortgage

In this technique, you pay cash for a property in order to purchase it at a substantial discount, then you take out a loan on the property to recover your cash. The net result is that you purchase the property without tying up your own cash for the long term. When you refinance you will recoup your cash—resulting in a no down payment deal.

Situation, Source(s), and Strategy

Ingredient	Description
Situation	You have cash available to you. The seller is in need of cash and is anxious to sell.
Source(s)	• Your available cash • An institutional or private lender
Strategy	Buy the seller's property at a substantial discount relative to its fair market value, then take out a loan on the property to recover your cash.

Example

You find a property that is worth $90,000 and will appraise for this amount. The seller needs to close quickly and is willing to accept less than market value for a cash offer. You have access to $80,000 cash. To use this technique, you would:

1. Offer to purchase the property for $75,000 cash with a quick closing date.

2. After the closing, obtain a loan amount equal to or greater than 90% of the appraised value.

When you finance the property you will recoup your purchase funds and closing costs, and you may even be able to borrow more than you paid.

Comments

If you and/or one or more partners have access to sizable amounts of cash, this technique is an outstanding way to purchase property. However, it requires that you find a seller who is in need of cash and is anxious to sell right away.

In one case, for example, I was contacted by a seller who needed to sell his property immediately, and was willing to sell at a substantial discount provided I pay all cash and close on the property within three days. Because I had an excellent relationship with a title insurance company and had some cash in the bank, I was able to do just that. I bought the property at a discount for approximately 75% of its fair market value. Then, by putting a new loan on the property, I was able to take out 100% of the cash that I had invested. Sometimes, after taking title to the property and making a few minor repairs, you can refinance the property, and take out even more cash than you invested.

Many professionals have cash available to invest under these types of circumstances, but they have neither the time nor expertise to search for and buy properties like this. If you can enter into a working relationship with just one or two such people, you can generate a good yearly cash flow for yourself, and for your investors as well.

Technique 15: Negotiate Discount Purchase of Distressed Properties

This technique requires that you acquire a physically distressed home, rehabilitate it, and put it on the market for a new appreciated value. Your decision to owner occupy the property should enable you to obtain a lower interest rate and overall better loan terms than if you were purchasing the property solely for investment purposes. When you sell the home, the profit you make is not taxed. The 1997 Tax Act provides that an individual can exclude a capital gain of up to $250,000 ($500,000 for a joint return) that is realized on the sale of a principal residence, if it was owned and used for a period of at least two years out of the last five years.

Situation, Source(s), and Strategy

Ingredient	Description
Situation	You want to purchase and rehabilitate a home and not pay taxes on the *capital gain* realized from selling the home.
Source(s)	• Institutional lender
Strategy	Negotiate, purchase, and then rehabilitate the home. (If you sell the home after two years, your gain of up to $250,000, or $500,000 if you file jointly, will be free.)

capital gain —Profit realized above the adjusted cost basis on the sale of property.

Example

You have found a physically distressed home for which the seller is asking $70,000. It will require $10,000 to rehabilitate the home, but in two years you estimate the rehabilitated home will be worth $120,000 based on appreciation and the fact that it is being sold below market now. To use this technique, you would:

1. Negotiate the purchase of the home for $60,000 using your credit or the credit or cash of an investor or equity partner.

2. Spend $10,000 to rehabilitate the home.

3. Sell the home for $120,000.

Your total profit at the end is $50,000 ($120,000 minus the $60,000 purchase price, minus the $10,000 cost of rehabilitating the home). If you have lived in the home for two years before selling, you pocket $50,000 tax free!

Comments

This technique is particularly attractive because of the tax advantages. You may also consider keeping the property and obtaining a refinancing loan to cash out some of the equity. The money you borrow is not taxed as income, and the interest you pay on the borrowed funds is tax deductible—once again demonstrating the incredible advantage of investing in real estate!

Technique 16: Use Investors and New First Mortgage

This technique involves joining with others to strengthen your loan approval capabilities. You may find that such a venture will enable you to get higher loan amounts or lower rates of interest—or both. The investor may cosign on the loan or take sole responsibility to provide you with the most desirable loan terms. The participation of each individual is open to negotiation and may be provided for in limitless ways.

Situation, Source(s), and Strategy

Ingredient	Description
Situation	You join with an investor whose income and/or credit help improve the loan terms you could not achieve alone.
Source	• Investor • Institutional lender
Strategy	Find an investor with credit or income that enables your purchase of a desired property.

Example

You find a bank-foreclosed home in a very desirable community that is listed considerably below its market value. The house is being offered for $185,000, but with minor cosmetic repairs could sell for $250,000 or more.

notes:

Your mortgage broker informs you that you have insufficient credit lines to be approved for more than 50% of the purchase price. The bank that owns the property refuses to sell the property on contract, extend a loan, or lease with option to buy.

You discuss this property with a fellow real estate investment club member. The investment club member is interested in partnering with you to make a profit on the eventual sale of the home. The member agrees to purchase the home for $185,000 and, in turn, lease the home to you with an option to buy for $220,000. It is also agreed that the member will request a $7,500 repair credit from the seller in the purchase offer. To use this technique, you would:

1. Locate an investment opportunity that will provide adequate compensation for you and an investor.

2. Partner with someone who is capable of obtaining or joining you in qualifying for desired loan terms.

Bank-owned properties are often sold below market value to achieve a quick sale. In this instance, you take advantage and receive instant equity and a no money down purchase.

Comments
The use of partners can open a wide range of real estate investment opportunities. I've dedicated Chapter 21, *Working With Partners*, to this subject. If properly structured, partnerships may be used with any of the techniques presented, and serve as a vehicle to help you close almost any transaction, regardless of size.

As with Technique 15, this technique allows you the opportunity to obtain this profit tax free if you occupy the property for two years prior to selling it.

Technique 17: Use Rental Participation
This technique involves offering the seller of an income property the chance to participate in any profits you might make by increasing rents—in exchange for his or her flexibility in terms and financing. Such flexibility can take various forms, including allowing you to purchase the property with no money down, financing the property by giving you a low-interest loan, or even offering you a *moratorium on interest* paid on such a loan.

Situation, Source(s), and Strategy

Ingredient	Description
Situation	You are purchasing an income property and want to persuade the seller to consider a flexible financing option.

> **moratorium on interest** — A time within the term of a loan during which it is permitted to delay payment of interest, or even not pay the interest at all.

notes:

Source(s)	• Future profits from the income property
	• The seller
Strategy	Offer the seller the chance to participate in future profits from rent increases, in exchange for his or her flexibility in your purchase of the property.

Example

You are negotiating to purchase a property that rents for $1,000 per month—that is, $12,000 per year ($1,000 times 12 months). To use this technique, you would:

- Offer to pay the seller a negotiated percentage (perhaps between 20% to 50%) of any annual rental income that exceeds $12,000 per year (excluding any forfeited security deposits) for a specified period of time, in exchange for a reduction in the down payment required on the property, a low-interest seller-financed loan, or a moratorium on interest paid on such a loan.

The seller's participation in future profits due to rent increases is a reward for his or her flexibility. In essence, the seller participates in the rewards of the property.

Comments

This technique is especially attractive to sellers with income property in need of repairs that are located in developing areas. If you can demonstrate to the seller that you are capable of making the needed repairs and increasing rents, they will likely welcome the opportunity to avoid the work while still participating in the future rents.

Technique 18: Use Land Contract

This technique calls for the purchaser to pay for all or most of the property before he or she receives legal title. In its simplest form, a land contract (also known as an agreement for deed, *contract for deed*, or installment contract) works like a mortgage, except that legal title does not pass to the purchaser until a specified number of payments have been made. This form of seller financing is quite popular in some parts of the country, yet practically unheard of in others. Theoretically, this technique provides additional protection for the seller in the event of default. If the purchaser does not make the payments as agreed, the land contract usually stipulates that the payments that have been made up to the date of default are forfeited. In most states, the seller is required to foreclose on the contract through a process similar to a mortgage foreclosure. This process affords some protection of the buyer's interest in the property. To provide notice of the agreement to the outside world, the land contract or an *Affidavit and Memorandum of Agreement* should be *recorded* in the public records. Because

contract for deed —A contract for the sale of real property wherein the seller is obligated to provide a merchantable title (a title free of liens and capable of being transferred) after the buyer has paid for the property, usually in installments.

record —The act of entering, in the public record, any instrument affecting title to real property.

notes:

states differ on the treatment and use of land contracts, I strongly recommend that you consult an attorney in your state to determine their appropriate use.

Land contracts specify the amount and number of the payments to be made. The payments are usually specified to be made monthly, with the money applied first to interest on the purchase price; second to charges such as real estate taxes, insurance, and special assessments, if any; and third to the unpaid principal balance of the purchase price. The contract might call for such payments to be made for any agreed-upon period of time—for example, 10 years, one year, or as little as 30 days—before legal title passes to the purchaser. If the contract states that the legal title will pass to the purchaser before the principal balance is paid in full, a balloon payment will usually become due. However, the seller can take back a note and mortgage in lieu of the balloon payment.

Situation, Source(s), and Strategy

Ingredient	Description
Situation	You want to buy a property with a mortgage that is not assumable for little or no money down. In addition, you might have bad credit. The seller is security minded, does not need to receive cash at closing, and is interested in receiving a regular monthly income.
Source(s)	• The seller
Strategy	Persuade the seller to accept a land contract on the property. Write the land contract so that it specifies that, after making regular payments for a specified period of time, you will take legal title to the property.

Example

You have found a two-unit property that is listed for $200,000 and on which there exists a first mortgage of $100,000. The monthly payment on the mortgage is $772. The owner is asking for a $30,000 cash down payment and has expressed a willingness to take back a wraparound mortgage for $170,000 at 9%. (For a description of wraparound mortgages, see the glossary and Technique 9.) Through negotiation, you have convinced the seller to accept $180,000 for the property. You know that you can rent both units for a total of $2,400 per month. To use this technique, you would:

1. Persuade the seller to sell you the property on a land contract.

2. Persuade the seller to take a $25,000 down payment in the form of six semi-annual payments of $4,167, each at 0% interest, beginning six

months from the date of the closing. This request is not unreasonable because a land contract protects a seller more than if he or she gave you legal title to the property at the time of closing.

3. Specify in the land contract that you will pay the seller $155,000 at 8% interest only, for five years, at the end of which time, you will take legal title to the property. Your monthly payments will be $1,033.

Even with the added monthly payment for taxes and insurance, which we will assume to be $567, your total cash out of pocket will be $1,600 per month. Since the rental income is $2,400 per month, you will have approximately $460 per month of positive cash flow even after subtracting a 10% management fee and a $100 per month cost for maintenance.

This transaction is clearly a win/win situation for both parties. You are buying the property with very little money down—in fact, with a security deposit and last-month rents from the tenants, you might even put cash in your pocket. The seller has received more than 90% of his or her asking price, has the security of knowing that he or she has not conveyed legal title of the property to you, and still has an income, including your semi-annual payments, of over $20,700 per year, which is roughly $1,700 per month.

Comments

If you use this technique to buy a property, keep in mind that if the contract for deed is for an extended period of time, for example 10 or 15 years, a number of events could take place that might put you, the buyer, in a precarious position.

condemnation —The process by which property of a private owner is taken, with or without consent, for public use. Fair compensation must be paid.

The land contract should address who will receive any fire insurance or *condemnation* proceeds. Also, to protect yourself from the sellers' divorcing, declaring bankruptcy, becoming mentally incompetent, or dying, you should have the seller execute a deed, and the deed should be held by a reputable third party. Your monthly payments should be mailed to the third party and, when the agreed-upon number of payments have been made, they will record the deed. For your protection, in the meantime, the third party might even make the monthly payment on the underlying first mortgage and remit the balance to the seller.

At the time you enter into the land contract, you should have a title search done to make certain the seller has clear title. Then, as mentioned earlier, after the contract has been signed, the contract itself or an *Affidavit and Memorandum of Agreement* should be recorded in the public records of the county where the property is located. It is also advisable to research the title again right before it is transferred to you.

notes:

Technique 19: Use Lease Option

This technique involves obtaining a lease on a property with the option to purchase the property in the future. This is one of the most cost-effective win/win purchase strategies. You can obtain the property with no money down and the seller will receive rent while awaiting payment of the option price. Because of the numerous opportunities this technique offers, I have dedicated the entire next Chapter 12, *Using Lease Options,* to a more thorough discussion of the concepts involved.

Situation, Source(s), and Strategy

Ingredient	Description
Situation	The seller wants to sell or is willing to rent.
Source(s)	• The seller • *Consideration* for the option to purchase.
Strategy	Negotiate a lease on the property with the option to purchase the property.

consideration —A thing of value (usually money) given as an inducement to enter a contract.

Example

The seller is willing to sell or lease a home that you estimate has a fair market value of $170,000. The seller will rent the home for $1,450 per month or sell for $160,000. To use this technique, you would:

- Offer a lease option paying $1,500 per month, with $500 per month counting as credit towards the purchase price of $160,000. The option may be exercised anytime within the first five years.

If you wait for five years to exercise your option, you will owe $130,000 ($160,000 purchase price less 60 months at $500, which equals $30,000). If the property increases in value 5% per year (the approximate national average over the last decade or so), it would be worth more than $200,000, based on the purchase price of $160,000.

Not a bad deal at all! You have in effect:

1. Bought the $160,000 home no money down. (You will have, however, probably put down a non-refundable "security deposit" as option consideration. This might represent one or two months' rent.)

2. Paid an "effective" interest rate of 7.5% ($1,000 per month times 12 equals $12,000, which, when divided by $160,000, equals 7.5%).

If, for some reason, at the end of the lease, you don't want to purchase the house (in the unlikely event that the home has gone down in value), you can simply "walk away" from the property.

Much more on these benefits and opportunities is discussed in Chapter 12, *Using Lease Options*.

Comments

Often lenders will accept the payments made on a lease option as evidence of rental or mortgage history. They may also take the payments into consideration to offset any required down payment. It is to your advantage to make timely payments on your lease, and keep diligent records of your payments to strengthen any future loan application.

Had the seller refused your offer of $160,000, rejected the terms you offered, and insisted on a $180,000 selling price, it might still have been an attractive investment. A financial analysis would have to be performed to make that determination.

REVIEW

Summary

The creative financing techniques presented in this chapter are proven! They have worked for me, and they've worked for thousands of my students. Your awareness and understanding of the techniques presented will allow you to recognize which opportunities best lend themselves to the use of each particular technique and combinations of techniques.

If you study the scenarios presented in this chapter closely, you will likely learn to spot future situations that are identical to the ones presented here. Many investors develop an expertise for spotting these specific investment scenarios and use the same proven solutions over and over.

Questions

- What is a wraparound mortgage? (See page 11-14.)

- What is a blanket mortgage, and how can it be used to buy real estate? (See page 11-15.)

- What is involved with the assumption of a loan? (See page 11-17.)

- What is rental participation, and how can it be used to purchase an income property? (See page 11-25.)

- What is a land contract? (See page 11-26.)

notes:

ACTION STEPS

To effectively employ creative financing techniques, you must educate yourself not only on what techniques are available, but also with regard to the options available to you personally. You should begin right now compiling information that will help you when it comes to inventing new techniques.

1. Check property advertisements and have a real estate broker or agent inform you of any properties that advertise seller financing.

2. Check with a mortgage broker and find out if you qualify for a loan program that allows seller financing.

3. Check for houses for rent in your area and see if the owners will lease with a purchase option.

FINAL COMMENTS

As you familiarize yourself with these strategies and their uses, keep in mind that the *Creative Options Guide*, which is included in your course materials, can help you to decide which strategies might apply to your situation. To use the guide, simply find the description that best fits the situation—go to the right-hand column, and find which financing options and strategies might work best for you.

With the right tools, any job is made easier. The techniques described in this chapter are the tools for success in real estate investment. But like the tools in your toolbox, they will not work if you don't use them. So I encourage you to study and master these techniques. Doing so will greatly assist you in reaching your goals.

NOTES

NOTES

OPTIONS

*"A lease with an option to purchase can be a **very profitable strategy** for making money in real estate. In general, it can help you purchase property with no money down and, at the same time, give you **immediate income**. And properly structured, a **lease option** is win/win—good for both the buyer and the seller.*

*One of my students has been **very successful** finding properties that need cosmetic work and asking for a six-month lease option. During this time period, he completes the work, rents the property, and finalizes the financing. At the end of six months, the property has **gained** significantly in **value**. And in the meantime, he has had a nice monthly **positive cash flow**."*

 *Carleton Sheets*

USING LEASE OPTIONS

Lease options, or lease purchase options as they are sometimes called, are powerful investing tools that can be used to create win/win situations for both buyers and sellers. With lease options, although you do not initially purchase the real estate, you do control it. As a buyer, a lease option can allow you to structure a no down payment deal that you can walk away from if you choose not to buy the property. Under the terms of a lease option, the portion of payments applied against the principal and the option consideration is considered tax-deferred income to the seller, until the option is exercised or its term expires. Common uses for lease options are to lease a personal residence or lease, and then sublease (known as a sandwich lease option), a residential or commercial investment property.

In this chapter, you will learn:

- What a lease option is and how it works.

- How a lease option can benefit both the buyer and the seller.

- How to use a sandwich lease option to your advantage.

- Why a lease option can be an outstanding way to acquire a dream residence of your own.

When you complete this chapter, you will be able to:

- Understand and use the *Residential Lease With Option to Purchase* form that I have included in the *Real Estate Forms Portfolio*.

- Identify what assets you already own that could be used as consideration for a lease option.

- Protect your rights as a buyer in a lease option.

notes:

WHAT IS A LEASE OPTION?

In simple terms, a lease option is a contract between a buyer and a seller that gives the buyer tenancy in a property, as well as the legal right to purchase the property at a predetermined price, or formula for price, on or before a specified future date. When you enter into a lease option with a seller, you promise to lease the property for a certain period of time and to make specified monthly payments. In return, the seller is obligated to sell the property to you under terms specified in the lease option agreement—if you choose to exercise your option.

To be effective, a lease option must be written and must include consideration—that is, something of value that the buyer gives to the seller in exchange for the seller's performance. The consideration is usually credited toward the purchase price at the time the option is exercised.

> *"There are many alternative forms of consideration that can be exchanged for the option to purchase. Be creative in meeting the seller's needs and you will have developed a great no down payment technique."*

Although most lease option contracts specify money as the consideration, you can use any number of things instead—for example, a mortgage on a property you already own, an unsecured promissory note, or even the written promise to pay the fix-up expenses for the property you're buying. The consideration could even be equity you have in some other property that you consider to be a dead asset or an asset that you no longer want, such as a time-share condominium, vacant land, a recreational vehicle, or a boat. For example, you own a time-share for which you paid $5,000 and find it difficult to sell. Perhaps this time-share could be used as consideration for a lease option.

Under the terms of a lease option, the *optionee* (buyer) is not required to exercise the option to buy the property on the specified future date. If the optionee does choose to exercise the option, however, the *optionor* (seller) is required to sell.

optionee —The person who has the legal right to purchase or not to purchase (through a contract) a specific property in the future.

THE BENEFITS OF LEASE OPTIONS

At first glance, it appears that a lease option only benefits the buyer. After all, the buyer is not obligated to buy the property, but if he or she chooses to do so, the seller is required to sell. If the lease option is carefully structured, however, it can be good for both the buyer and the seller.

Benefits for the Buyer (Optionee)
For the buyer, the major benefits of a lease option are these:

optionor —The seller of a property who extends an option to a potential buyer. If the optionee exercises the option, the optionor is legally bound to sell. However, if the option is not exercised, then the optionor is released from any obligation.

notes:

- The risk is low, and the financial leverage can be high.

- The buyer can walk away from the contract if the value of the property on the specified future date does not justify its purchase at the agreed-upon price.

- The buyer receives control and possession of the property.

- Very little, or no, initial closing costs.

Option consideration is usually small compared to the value of the property. Therefore, the buyer risks very little and can end up controlling a large property having put practically no money down. This is truly great financial leverage for the buyer.

When a buyer enters into a lease option with a seller, he or she is betting that the value of the property on a specified future date will be greater than the agreed-upon purchase price or, if not, that considerable equity may be achieved as a result of the credits of some or all of the monthly payments from the purchase price. If the buyer is right, then by purchasing the property at the specified date and price, he or she will gain instant equity. If, however, the value of the property on the specified future date is less than the specified purchase price, the buyer can walk away from the contract, or attempt to renegotiate the price.

A lease option gives the buyer both control and possession of a property. The buyer gets the benefits of occupying or subleasing the property and perhaps even improving it to increase its value. The buyer can even generate profit from the property by leasing it to someone else.

Benefits for the Seller (Optionor)
The seller can also benefit from a well-structured lease option. Here are a few of the ways that can happen:

- The agreed-upon price of the property is frequently at the top of its current market value range.

- The option money that the seller receives is tax-deferred, until exercised or expired.

- The option is forfeited if rent is not paid on time.

- The seller receives all the equity buildup (amortization) on the mortgage during the option period.

notes:

- The tenant has pride of ownership and, therefore, an incentive to take good care of the property.

- The rent, including the amount, if any, that is applicable to the option purchase price, is at the top of, or above, the fair market rental range.

- The ability to regain possession and control of the property in the event of the optionee's default in meeting the terms of the agreement.

When a buyer and seller agree to a lease option, they must set the purchase price of the property in the contract. Typically, the set price might be at the very top of the current market value range that applies to the property. In fact, depending on the length of the option period, it can even be higher. This higher price compensates the seller for a potential increase in the value of the property due to appreciation of value.

If the purchase price is based on a formula rather than a fixed price, the lease option can be structured so that the seller shares in any increase in the property's value over the term of the option agreement. Many options that are structured this way tie the purchase price to cost-of-living increases or a rate of inflation. Others specify that an appraisal will be performed at a particular time by two appraisers, and that the purchase price will be the average of the appraised values. (In general, I feel it is best to set a specific price at the time you first negotiate the option.)

One other benefit to the seller is that the portion of the payment applicable to the purchase price is tax-deferred. This applies to money received both as a lump sum at contract signing (option consideration) and on a continuing monthly basis (rent credits). No tax is due on that money until the option is either exercised or forfeited at the end of the contract term. If the buyer exercises the option, any money received by the seller is treated as a capital gain or ordinary income, depending upon the seller's tax situation, how long the seller has owned the property, and whether or not it was the seller's principle residence.

> *"If carefully structured, an option can be good for both the buyer and the seller—a true win/win situation."*

If the buyer chooses not to exercise the option, the money that has been paid to the seller is treated as ordinary income. So the seller benefits either way, because he or she gets the untaxed use of the option money for a period of time.

notes:

> *premium* —An additional sum of money paid as an incentive for someone to do something.

Also, during the option period, the seller retains ownership of the property; therefore, he or she receives all of the tax benefits from owning the property as well as any equity buildup on any existing mortgages. Some lease options are even structured so that the buyer's option consideration does not apply toward the purchase price of the property. When this happens, the extra money that the seller receives is simply a *premium*. Even though the seller retains ownership of the property, the buyer has a strong incentive to take good care of the property that he or she might someday own.

Finally, if the option is structured correctly, the seller never has to worry about whether or not he or she will receive payments on time. Most options specify that the option is forfeited if the rent is not paid on a timely basis; therefore, buyers almost always make sure that rent is paid in a timely manner. Also, the rent, including option payments, is usually set at or above the fair market rent for the property.

Many sellers structure a lease option so that it is two separate documents, a lease and an option to purchase. They feel that by separating the two, it is easier to evict the tenant for default under the lease terms without consideration of the credits the tenant-purchaser has earned under the terms of the two documents. Both documents must contain a cross-default clause that specifies that the default on one document is a default on both. As an investor, who is a sublessor giving a tenant the right to lease the property with an option to buy, the same rationale would apply.

WAYS TO USE LEASE OPTIONS

There are many creative ways to use lease options. The most common uses of the lease option are:

- Lease optioning a property with the intent to sublease to another person with a purchase option (sandwich lease).

- Lease optioning a personal residence.

- Lease optioning a property requiring modest rehabilitation to sell to an end user or keep as a rental.

The lease option can be used on commercial investment properties as well as residential or investment properties.

notes:

> "Conditions are
> never just right.
> People who delay
> action until all fac-
> tors are favorable
> do nothing."
>
> ~William Feather

The following is a real-life example, with actual numbers, of a lease option from one of my students that extended over a five-year period. Needless to say, the lease option agreement was entered into several years ago, but the principles and the economics of the transaction are very much applicable today.

The buyer (my student) owned a house worth roughly $100,000, which was typical of the home values in most of the surrounding neighborhoods and towns. There were a fair number of rental homes in the area; most of them rented in the $500 to $700 range. Seeking to find a substantially nicer home, the buyer sought out a nearby upscale town where the home values exceeded $200,000. Rentals in this upscale area were fairly scarce.

The buyer found a lovely home for sale for $220,000, and it appeared that it was reasonably priced. The seller was very anxious to sell in that he had already moved out of state, and the home had now been on the market for several months. The buyer proposed a lease option, and they ended up agreeing to a four-year option at the asking price of $220,000. The monthly rent was $900 (low for this particular house, but high in comparison to almost all other rentals in the surrounding areas), and the buyer received a 50% rent credit ($450 per month) toward the eventual purchase. The seller was to pay taxes and insurance during the option period, and the buyer agreed to pay for all of the maintenance (an inspection revealed that the house was in very good shape). The buyer put down $3,600 as a nonrefundable deposit for the option consideration, which was equivalent to less than 2% of the option purchase price!

As the years went on, the buyer was delighted with his fine new home, and was equally delighted with the affordability of the new home. He was paying an equivalent monthly payment of $450 (1/2 of $900) compared to the previous monthly payment of $840 for principal, interest, taxes, and insurance (commonly called PITI) on his previous home which, you will recall, was worth less than half of his new home!

My student (the buyer) was amazed when he figured out the "effective" interest rate that he was paying. He realized, that of the $900 a month he was paying, only $450 of that was not going toward the purchase price. And from that, he subtracted the cost of taxes and insurance (which were $340 per month—an amount he would have had to pay had he owned the property) to yield a net "cost" of $110 a month. This worked out to an incredible effective interest rate of 0.6% ($110 times 12 months equals $1,320, divided by $220,000, which equals 0.6%). That's less than 1%!

After three years, the buyer was certain that he was going to exercise his option at the end of the four-year period (because, among other reasons, property values had been increasing very nicely in this area—at about 7% per year), but he figured it was worth the effort to see if the seller would be willing to extend the option in exchange for some additional consideration. The buyer and seller ended up agreeing to extend the option for one additional year in return for the buyer paying $10,000 of additional option consideration (which meant that it would be fully applied to the purchase price, but it would be forfeited if the buyer did not buy the house). Was this a good move? I sure think so. Even if it cost the buyer 10% interest to borrow the $10,000 for a year (which is $1,000), that was a small price to pay for another year of ownership at the effective interest rate of under 1%.

After the five-year period, the buyer exercised the option and obtained the necessary funds by simply obtaining an owner-occupied loan (loan programs specifically designed for owner-occupants) for $179,400, which was the total amount due to the seller ($220,000 less the deposit of $3,600, less the additional consideration of $10,000 paid in year four, and less the rent credit of $27,000 which is equal to $450 for 60 mo. or 5 years). The property appreciated and it appraised for $290,000; thus the new loan that was obtained was for only 62% of the property's fair market value. (By the way, the buyer eventually sold this house about a year later for $320,000 and, you guessed it, has since moved on to an even nicer home!)

The buyer's "profit" was $90,000, based on this initial investment of $3,600, property appreciation of $70,000 plus a $20,400 savings of not having to pay taxes and insurance while living in the house. Under a lease option like this, the buyer (and seller, in this case) benefited in that the real estate taxes remained fairly steady throughout the five-year period because there had not been a reported sale of the property.

The action that the buyer took at the end of year three (asking for and getting the seller to agree to an additional year extension) is an excellent example of the power of creative thinking. This would have been a great investment even if that had not occurred, but by thinking creatively and being willing to ask, the buyer turned what was already a great investment into one that was even better!

It is very easy to find homes that a buyer would be interested in. In this case, the buyer was leaving a $100,000 home and was looking at homes that were more than twice as "expensive" as what he already had. As you can imagine, just about any property that is more than twice as expensive as what you already have will almost assuredly meet your needs, and then some! Therefore, just about every home on the market in these higher price ranges is a candidate, and it sure does make "house-hunting" a lot more fun when you can open up the possibilities like this. A lot of offers can be made, and it only takes one "yes!"

Let's take a look at how the buyer and the seller fared over this five-year deal. Table 12.1 shows the benefits for both the buyer and the seller:

Table 12.1: Lease Option Example—Benefits for the Buyer and the Seller

Benefits to the Buyer	Benefits to the Seller
• Flexibility of option to purchase any time within a four-year term (this option was additionally extended for one more year).	• The seller received full asking price.
• Out of the total monthly rental payment of $900, $450 is credited toward the purchase. Thus, effectively the cost of occupancy is $450 a month.	• The seller is relieved of all maintenance responsibility and cost associated with the property. • The seller receives sufficient income to cover the property taxes, insurance, and the principal and interest payment on the existing mortgage, plus a monthly profit.
• Initial down payment of $3,600 and subsequent option extension of $10,000 are credited directly against the purchase price.	• The seller receives a nonrefundable deposit up front. • The seller retains the $54,000 in rent payments ($900 per month rent payment) and $13,600 total option deposit if the buyer fails to exercise the option and pay the entire purchase price. If he exercises the option, the seller credits back these amounts against the purchase price.
• The buyer had the advantage of time to put himself in the position to buy a home that he may not otherwise have been able to afford.	
• Based on appreciation of approximately 7% per year, the buyer will enjoy instant equity of $110,600 ($290,000 fair market value minus $179,400 option purchase price balance).	• The seller enjoys the reduction of the loan principal which increases the amount the seller will cash out at closing or the equity the seller will have in the property if the buyer does not complete the transaction.
• The buyer will have a much easier time obtaining favorable loan terms with $110,600 in equity in the property and therefore needs a mere 62% LTV (loan to value) to pay off the balance of the option purchase price.	• The seller enjoys the deferment of taxes on the portion of money applied to the option purchase price (including the $3,600 and the $10,000 consideration) until the option is exercised or abandoned. • The seller has the peace of mind of knowing that the property is under contract and is being maintained by someone motivated to take good care of it because, hopefully, they will soon own it.

While it may be difficult to find sellers who will accept a transaction that is this favorable to the buyer, let's see what would have happened under other circumstances. If the seller would have restricted the option period to just 24 months with no extensions and allowed only $250 rent credit to apply against the $220,000 purchase price, the tenant/buyer would still have a pretty good deal.

In this instance, the tenant/buyer's return on his initial investment of $3,600 (option consideration) would have been $41,478 (appreciation of $31,878 plus the option consideration of $3,600 and rent credit of $6,000). The buyer could pay the balance due on the option purchase contract of $210,400 ($220,000 purchase price minus $3,600 option consideration and $6,000 rent credit) by obtaining a loan value of less than 85% (85% of the property's value of $251,900 is $214,115).

notes:

> *sublease* —The leasing of leased property by the lessee to another person.

Either of these alternatives are perfect examples of how a lease option can be very powerful for the buyer, and yet still represent an attractive proposition for the seller.

Lease Option Combined With a Sublease Purchase Option on a Residential Property

One way to make money using lease options is to enter into a lease option contract with an anxious seller and a *sublease* option contract with an anxious buyer—for example, a buyer who might not be able to qualify for conventional financing. This technique is referred to as a sandwich lease option. Here's an example of how it might work—

Assume that you find a property that fits your investment profile and has a current fair market value of $180,000. The seller purchased the property seven years ago for $127,000 with a down payment of $7,000 and acquired a 30-year mortgage loan at 8% interest on the remaining $120,000. His monthly mortgage loan payments, insurance, and real estate taxes are $882, $48, and $200, respectively—which results in a total monthly payment of $1,130.

After some negotiation, you acquire control of the property by agreeing with the seller to a four-year lease option contract under which you will pay $1,130 per month in rent, and you reserve the right to purchase the home for its fair market value of $180,000 at anytime during the lease term. You also reserve the right to sublease the property and offer a $500 promissory note as your consideration. The $500 note will be applied toward the $180,000 purchase price if you purchase the property. If you don't exercise the option and purchase the property, you will need to pay off the $500 note.

> *"Make sure that the right to assign is spelled out in the lease option contract."*

Once you have gained control of the property, you find a tenant who is willing to enter into a sublease option contract on the property. You offer a two-year term on the contract under which the tenant pays $4,500 in consideration, and $1,700 per month in rent, $100 of which is credited toward a purchase price of $200,000 at the end of the lease term. Under the terms of the contract, you gain a positive total monthly cash flow of $570 ($1,700 minus $1,130 rent) for 24 months, which amounts to a total of about $13,700 over the contract term.

If the tenant exercises his option to purchase at the end of the sublease term, he pays $200,000 minus the $2,400 in credit he has accumulated over two years (24 times $100), minus the $4,500 that he paid as consideration to enter into the contract. As a result, his total purchase price is $193,100 ($200,000 minus $2,400, minus $4,500). If the fair market value of the home increases at 5% over the sublease term, its value at the end of the two years is $198,000, which results in $4,900 ($198,000 minus $193,100) equity for the tenant when he

notes:

becomes the new owner. (If the tenant does not exercise the option to purchase, you still have 24 months to find another prospective tenant/buyer, and you might be able to make even more money on the property.)

The key to using this technique profitably and without risk is to secure a tenant (that is, a subtenant) prior to making the original commitment for the lease option on the property. Table 12.2 shows how the transaction works out for the parties involved:

Table 12.2: Results of Sandwich Lease Option Example

Party	Item	Amount
Seller	Sale proceeds (from you)	$180,000
	Cash flow (2 years)	0
	Principal amortized (2 years)	3,200
	Total to original seller	$183,200*
You	Sale proceeds (from tenant)	$193,100
	Sublease option consideration	4,500
	Cash flow	13,700
	Total income due to sublease/purchase contract	$211,300
	Purchase price (total to original seller)	(180,000)
	Total profit to you (2 years)	$31,300
Tenant	New home value	$198,000
	Purchase price (to you)	(193,100)
	Total new owner equity	$4,900

*Gross-existing mortgage must be paid off.

This example illustrates just one way to make money with lease options. You could also fulfill the obligation of the original lease option and buy the property to use as a rental property. You could also sell the original option to another investor.

Lease Option With the Right to Sublease a Large Investment/Commercial Property

Lease option agreements are also useful in commercial purchases. The size and cost of many commercial properties place them beyond the reach of many investors who lack creativity. As a result, the sellers of large apartment buildings, strip malls, and warehouses find themselves having to list these properties on the market for prolonged periods of time. In some cases these properties are vacant and producing no income.

notes:

The lease option with the right to sublease allows creative investors to take over commercial properties for little or no money down. Through quality property management decisions, these properties can be subleased at a sizable profit, sold at a price substantially greater than the option purchase price, or the option could be sold and assigned. The lease option buyer receives the additional benefit of managing the property before actually purchasing it. In this way the buyer is given a real estate management test-drive that will result in a more educated purchase decision.

> *"You should always attempt to negotiate an extension provision in all options because you might need additional time to purchase the property."*

PROTECTING YOURSELF WHEN USING LEASE OPTIONS

If you enter into a lease option agreement without taking special care to protect yourself, you might find that the specific terms of the lease option are so binding that it is almost impossible to exercise. To protect yourself, you must make sure to record the option and to retain important rights when you structure the option.

Recording the Option

Whenever you enter into an option agreement with a seller, you should either record the option or, if you want the terms of the option to remain confidential, record an *Affidavit and Memorandum of Agreement* in the public records of the county where the property is located. This document (the *Affidavit and Memorandum of Agreement*) notifies the world that there is a pending sale, or at least an agreement that could affect the real estate in question, but does not disclose the terms of the agreement. I have included a form in my *Real Estate Forms Portfolio* for your convenience.

Retaining Important Rights

As a buyer, you need to make sure that you are aware of your rights when you enter into an option agreement and that they are spelled out clearly in the contract. You should especially try to retain the right to sublease, the right to *assign*, and the right to extend.

assign —To transfer one's rights in a bond, mortgage, lease, or other legal instrument to another person.

Right to Sublease

Whether you plan to live in the property or not, you should always attempt to have your lease option give you the right to sublease the property to another tenant (you may find this difficult to do, and somewhat unnecessary, if you are using a lease option on an "upper bracket" home that you will live in). That right is not inherent in a lease unless it is spelled out. The *Residential Lease With Option to Purchase* form, included in the *Real Estate Forms Portfolio*, specifically gives you the right to sublease.

notes:

Right to Assign

Assignment is the right to transfer the contract and all of your rights to someone else. In some states, the right to assign a contract is protected by law. In other states, it is not. You should always make sure that the right to assign the contract is spelled out in your lease option contract to avoid any misunderstanding or litigation later on. If you choose not to exercise the option yourself, you should retain the right to sell the option to someone else. If you don't retain that right, you forfeit the payments being applied to the sale price as well as an option consideration.

The seller also benefits by providing you with the right to assign the contract because, if you choose not to exercise the option, he or she does not have to find another buyer for the property. As you would expect, the lease option contract provided in the *Real Estate Forms Portfolio* retains your right to assign.

Right to Extend

Some lease option contracts include a section that spells out the terms under which the option can be extended. This is known as an *extension clause.* Other contracts specifically say that the extension of the lease option is prohibited. Still other contracts are silent on this point. Regardless of what your lease option says or does not say, give careful consideration to try and retain the right to extend the option period for at least one year. This extension clause can be added to the lease option contract or, if space is a problem, onto an addendum.

You should be aware that the right to extend can be expensive. Try to structure your contract so that you only incur this "cost" (such as a higher option price, or additional option consideration to be paid) if and when you choose to extend the contract. It is important to have this "additional option" to extend the term so that you protect yourself from losing all of the credit that you have built up.

> *extension clause* —A clause in a contract that lists the terms under which an agreement can be extended.

UNDERSTANDING THE LEASE OPTION CONTRACT

The *Residential Lease With Option to Purchase* form included in the *Real Estate Forms Portfolio* provides an excellent lease option contract. Figure 12.1(a,b) shows an example of a personal residence lease option contract. Remember, because this form is designed to apply in many situations, some of the sections may not correspond to your needs. Depending upon each situation, simply cross out those sections that are inappropriate. Also, when preparing the contract make sure that it's legible and typed or clearly printed. Doing so protects both you and the seller.

Provisions

Let's take a look at several important parts of the *Residential Lease With Option to Purchase* form. (Refer to Figure 12.1(a,b) for numbers referred to in this section.)

notes:

lessor —One who rents property under a lease (also know as a landlord).

lessee —One who contracts to hold occupancy rights in the real property of another (also known as a tenant).

legal description —The means to identify the exact boundaries of a property. A surveyor will use the recorded plats method, metes and bounds method, or the government survey method to describe real property.

Date and Names

Fill in the date of the contract and the name of the owner, who is referred to as "*lessor*" throughout the contract. Fill in your name in the blank for "*lessee*." Note that the words "and/or assigns" give you the right to assign the contract at any time.

Total Deposit

Fill in the total deposit amount. This amount is generally the option consideration plus one month's rent. Whatever the amount, spell it out. The larger the amount, the more attractive your offer is to the lessor.

Property Address and Legal Description

Fill in the address of the property covered by the lease option along with a *legal description* of the property.

Property General Description

Briefly describe the property in this space—for example, "three-unit apartment building" or "single-family residence located at 101 S. Elm, Anywhere, USA."

Paragraph 1: Personal Property

List all personal property you want to be included in this lease option—for example, "washer, dryer, all window treatments, riding lawn mower, freezer in basement."

Paragraph 2: Term

Write the date when the lease option begins and the number of months that it will remain in effect.

Paragraph 3: Rent

Rent is the total amount of money that you are to pay each month to the owner. Fill in the address where the rent should be paid and the penalty for late rent checks.

Paragraph 4: Utilities, Taxes, and Insurance

You will be responsible for all utilities except those that you list in this space. Your form provides that the lessor is responsible for paying the real estate taxes and insurance. The lessor may object to this, but it is surely worth asking for.

Paragraph 5: Use

"Use" refers to your intended use—for example, "residential occupancy."

Paragraph 7: Assignment and Subletting

This short paragraph is powerful and important. It gives you the right to both assign and sublet the lease option.

Paragraph 10: Possession

This clause protects you in the event that the owner does not give you possession of the property by the date specified. Prior and subsequent to this period, you are not required to pay rent and you are not bound by the contract.

notes:

Paragraph 11: Security/Option Consideration

Fill in the amount of the security deposit. You might offer a larger security deposit to increase the chance of having your lease option contract accepted by the owner, especially for long-term option periods (three to five years). A security deposit (option consideration) of several thousand dollars makes your offer much more attractive to the owner.

If the lump-sum payment of a large security deposit is not possible for you, ask the seller to allow you to spread the amount over a period of time, say 12 to 18 months. Even with $6,000 as a security deposit for a long-term lease option, you still have an outstanding investment. When you exercise the option, the security deposit is usually treated as a credit against the purchase price. This should be spelled out in the contract.

Paragraph 16: Time

Fill in the date. Allow only one day for the owner to accept the contract.

Paragraph 18: Default

This paragraph states that the lessee has three days, from the time written notice of default is received from the lessor, to cure the default and avoid legal default and the loss of his or her option rights.

Paragraph 19: Option

Spell out the terms of the option agreement in this section. Show the full price of the property that you agree to pay the seller at the end of the lease term.

Paragraph 21: Examination of Title

You have 15 days from the date the option is exercised to examine the owner's title to the property. The lessor is required to show you evidence of title by providing a title insurance policy.

Paragraph 26: Expiration of Option

Enter the expiration date of the lease option. Note that the lease option can be exercised at any time prior to the expiration date.

> *"Paragraph 27 can be the most important paragraph in the entire document. You should almost always plan on a minimum 10% to 20% rent credit. It is not unheard of to have 50% or more of your rent credited to the purchase price."*

Paragraph 27: Exercise of Option

Fill in the blank with the percentage of rent paid that is to be credited to the purchase price.

Signatures

To make the contract legally binding, both parties must sign and date it.

RESIDENTIAL LEASE WITH OPTION TO PURCHASE

THIS AGREEMENT made and entered into on this __1st__ day of (mo.) __September__ (yr.) __2004__ by and between __Lee Landlord__ hereinafter called Lessor and __Teresa Tenant__ and/or assigns, hereinafter called Lessee: The Lessor, for and in consideration of the sum of __$3,000.__ dollars in hand paid by the Lessee, receipt of which is hereby acknowledged, hereby leases to Lessee, his/her heirs or assignees, the premises situated in the City of __Anywhere__ County of __Guessit__ State of __Il.__, legally described as____ (See Legal) _____

_____.

(If the legal description is not included at the time of execution, it may be attached to and incorporated herein afterward.)
(Street Address: __435 Garfield St. Anywhere, Illinois__) and consisting of __single family resident__ upon the following TERMS and CONDITIONS:

1. Personal Property: Said lease shall include the following personal property: __Stove, refrigerator, dishwasher, all window treat-treatments and all the furniture in the recreation room.__ _____.

2. Term: The term hereof shall commence on (mo./day) __October 1__ , (yr.) __2004__, and continue for a period of __36__ months thereafter.

3. Rent: Rent shall be $ __1,300.__ per month, payable in advance, upon the first day of each calendar month to Lessor or his/her authorized agent at the following address: __117 Main Street Anywhere, Illinois__ or at such other places as may be designated by Lessor from time to time. In the event rent is not paid within five (5) days after due date, Lessee agrees to pay a late charge of $ __25 per day__ plus interest at __9__ % per annum on the delinquent amount.

4. Utilities; Taxes, and Insurance: Lessee shall be responsible for the payment of all utilities and services except __no exceptions__ which shall be paid by the Lessor. Lessor shall be responsible for the payment of real estate taxes and insurance on the property.

5. Use: The premises shall be used as a residence and for no other purpose without prior written consent of Lessor.

6. House Rules: In the event that the premises are in a building containing more than one unit, Lessee agrees to abide by any and all house rules, whether promulgated before or after the execution hereof, including, but not limited to, rules with respect to noise, odors, disposal of refuse, pets, parking, and use of common areas.

7. Assignment and Subletting: Lessee may assign this agreement or sublet any portion of the premises.

8. Maintenance, Repairs, or Alterations: Lessee shall maintain the premises in a clean and sanitary manner including all equipment, appliances, furniture and furnishings therein, and shall surrender the same at termination thereof, in as good condition as received, normal wear and tear excepted. Lessee shall be responsible for damages caused by his/her negligence and that of his/her family, or invitees or guests. Lessee shall maintain any surrounding grounds, including lawns and shrubbery, and keep the same clear of rubbish and weeds, if such grounds are part of the premises and are exclusively for use of the Lessee.

9. Entry and Inspection: Lessee shall permit Lessor or Lessor's agents to enter the premises at reasonable times and upon reasonable notice for the purpose of inspecting the premises or for making necessary repairs.

10. Possession: If Lessor is unable to deliver possession of the premises at the commencement hereof, Lessor shall not be liable for any damage caused thereby nor shall this agreement be void or voidable, but Lessee shall not be liable for any rent until possession is delivered. Lessee may terminate this agreement if possession is not delivered within __30__ days of the commencement of the term hereof.

11. Security/Option Consideration: The security deposit of $ __600.__ shall secure the performance of the Lessee's obligations hereunder. Lessor may, but shall not be obligated to, apply all or portions of said deposit on account of Lessee's obligations hereunder. Any balance remaining upon termination shall be returned to Lessee.

12. Deposit Funds: Any returnable deposits shall be refunded within fifteen (15) days from the date possession is delivered to Lessor or his/her authorized agent.

13. Attorney Fees: The prevailing party shall be entitled to all costs incurred in connection with any legal action brought by either party to enforce the terms hereof or relating to the demised premises, including reasonable attorneys' fees.

14. Notices: Any notice which either party may or is required to give, may be given by mailing the same, postage prepaid, to Lessee or at such other places as may be designated by the parties from time to time.

15. Heirs, Assigns, Successors: This lease and option shall include and insure to and bind the heirs, executors, administrators, successors, and assigns of the respective parties hereto.

16. Time: Time is of the essence of this agreement. This offer shall terminate if not accepted before (mo./day) __6pm, September 1__ (yr.) __2004__.

17. Holding Over: Any holding over after expiration of the term of this lease, with the consent of the Lessor, shall be construed as a month-to-month

Figure 12.1(a): *Residential Lease With Option to Purchase* form, Side 1

tenancy in accordance with the terms hereof, as applicable.

18. Default: If Lessee shall fail to pay rent when due or perform any term hereof after not less than three (3) days written notice of such default given in the manner required by law, the Lessor at his/her option may terminate all rights of the Lessee hereunder, unless Lessee, within said time, shall cure such default. If Lessee abandons or vacates the property while in default of payment of rent, Lessor may consider any property left on premises to be abandoned and may dispose of the same in any manner allowed by law. In the event the lessor reasonably believes that such abandoned property has no value, it may be discarded.

19. Option: Lessee shall have the option to purchase the leased premises described herein upon the following TERMS and CONDITIONS:

  a. The total purchase price shall be $ _150,000._ (_One hundred and fifty thousand_ dollars)

  b. The purchase price shall be paid as follows:

  Cash at Closing

20. Encumbrances: Lessee shall take title to the property subject to: 1) Real Estate Taxes not yet due and 2) Covenants, conditions, restrictions, reservations, rights, rights of way, and easements of record, if any.

21. Examination of Title: Lessee shall have fifteen (15) days from the date of receipt of title report to examine the title to the property and to report, in writing, any valid objections thereto. Any exceptions to the title which would be disclosed by examination of the records shall be deemed to have been accepted unless reported in writing within said fifteen (15) days. If Lessee objects to any exceptions to the title, Lessor shall use all due diligence to remove such exceptions at his/her own expense within sixty (60) days thereafter. But if such exceptions cannot be removed within the sixty (60) days allowed, all rights and obligations hereunder may, at the election of the Lessee, terminate and end unless he/she elects to purchase the property subject to such exceptions.

22. Evidence of Title: Lessor shall provide evidence of Title in the form of a policy of title insurance at Lessor's expense.

23. Bill of Sale: The personal property identified in paragraph _one_ shall be conveyed by bill of sale.

24. Closing: Closing shall be within _45_ days from exercise of the option unless otherwise extended by other terms of this agreement.

25. Prorations: Tax and insurance escrow account, if any, to be transferred intact to Lessee with no prorations. Interest and other expenses of the property to be prorated as of the date of closing. Unpaid real estate taxes, security deposits, advance rentals, or considerations involving future lease credits shall be credited to the Lessee.

26. Expiration of Option: This option may be exercised at any time prior to its expiration at midnight *(mo./day)* _October 1_ , *(yr.)* _2004_. Upon expiration, Lessor shall be released from all obligations hereunder and all of Lessee's rights hereunder, legal or equitable, shall cease.

27. Exercise of Option: The option shall be exercised by mailing or delivering written notice to the Lessor prior to the expiration of this option. Notice, if mailed, shall be by certified mail, postage prepaid, to the Lessor at the address set forth below, and shall be deemed to have been given upon the day shown on the postmark of the envelope in which such notice is mailed. In the event the option is exercised, _25%_ percent of the rent paid hereunder, as well as any security deposit paid, prior to the exercise of the option shall be credited upon the purchase price.

28. Right To Sell: Lessor warrants to Lessee that Lessor is the legal owner of the leased premises and has the legal right to sell leased premises under the terms and conditions of this agreement.

IN WITNESS WHEREOF, the parties hereto have executed this agreement the day and year first above written.

Teresa Tenant

LESSEE

Lee Laudord

LESSOR

LESSEE

2113 Washington St. Apt #7

Anywhere, Illinois

ADDRESS

LESSOR

117 Main Street

Anywhere, Illinis

ADDRESS

Figure 12.1(b): *Residential Lease With Option to Purchase* Form, Side 2

notes:

REVIEW

Summary

A lease option is a legal right that a seller gives to a buyer to rent and purchase property at a predetermined price or formula for price on, or before, a specified future date. Lease options provide benefits to both buyers and sellers. For example, a buyer can use a lease option to structure a low, or no money down deal and exercise the option to purchase or walk away at the end of the option term. Lease options can benefit sellers in a variety of ways, including providing tax-deferred income. The most common uses for lease options are purchasing or subleasing a personal residence or investment property.

Every option must be supported by consideration. The consideration usually takes the form of money, but can also be items like an unsecured promissory note, or equity in another property that you own.

When you enter into a lease option, you should always try to make sure that the agreement gives you the right to sublease, the right to assign, and the right to extend. The right to extend might increase the cost of the lease, but it can protect you from losing all the credits you have accumulated. Note, however, that your inability to obtain one or more of these rights does not necessarily mean you should walk away from what still may be a great deal.

The *Residential Lease With Option to Purchase* form is both a formal way to present your offer and a legal contract. This form spells out all the details of the lease option, including facts on security deposits, possession, personal property, and rents. To protect yourself, this form or an *Affidavit and Memorandum of Agreement* should be recorded in the county records where the property being purchased is located.

Questions

- What is a lease option?
  (See page 12-1.)

- What are three nonmonetary items that can be used for option consideration? (See page 12-1.)

- What three rights should you attempt to retain when entering into a lease option agreement with a seller? (See page 12-10.)

- How many days should you allow an owner to accept the lease option contract? (See page 12-13.)

notes:

ACTION STEPS

1. Using the scenario under the section *Ways to Use Lease Options*, complete a copy of the *Residential Lease With Option to Purchase* form. This will verify your understanding of the lease option techniques and prepare you for your first transaction.

2. Make a list of items that you could possibly offer a potential seller as consideration for a lease option.

FINAL COMMENTS

With lease options, you do not initially purchase the real estate, you control it; however, lease options can provide you with a very profitable strategy for making money in real estate. If you ultimately decide not to exercise your option, you can potentially sell your option to another investor for cash. If buying the property at the end of the lease term is not right for your situation, you can just walk away.

NOTES

NOTES

NEGOTIATE

*"In my 30-plus years of **negotiating,** I have learned that both parties must be **happy** about the **outcome** of a transaction to consider it a success. And on the surface, that shouldn't be too difficult. Let's face it, you have a common goal—you both want a mutually **beneficial result**.*

*But to **achieve** this, you and the seller must maintain a **cordial atmosphere,** exchange ideas, and of course, sometimes make **concessions**. Finding a common ground with the other party is very important."*

Carleton Sheets

13

MAKING THE OFFER AND NEGOTIATING

All real estate transactions involve negotiation. Successful negotiation always results in a winning situation for both the buyer and the seller. A good negotiator adopts a win/win style, establishes trust and credibility to create a positive negotiating environment, and is always diplomatic and respectful.

To prepare for a negotiation you must evaluate your needs as well as those of the other party. Only then are you ready to develop an appropriate strategy for the negotiations. There are various ways to make an offer that will ensure a successful transaction. Each type of offer has advantages and disadvantages for the buyer and seller. You must determine which offer is best for your situation.

In this chapter, you will learn:

- How to use a negotiation checklist.

- How to use a win/win negotiation strategy.

- How to prepare for and conduct a negotiation, including evaluating the needs of the buyer and the seller, and developing a negotiation strategy.

- How to make the appropriate offer based on your specific situation.

When you complete this chapter, you will be able to:

- Confidently prepare for and conduct a win/win negotiation.

- Make intelligently crafted offers when buying property.

WHAT YOU NEED TO KNOW TO NEGOTIATE

To successfully negotiate with a seller, you must know the property and understand all aspects of your own situation, as well as, to the best of your ability, the seller's situation. In particular, you need to understand not only what a seller wants, but also why he or she wants it. Only then can you know how to best approach the seller and what kind of offer he or she might accept.

THE BASICS OF NEGOTIATION

For a real estate negotiation to be considered successful, both the buyer and the seller must be satisfied with the outcome of the negotiation, and each party must believe that he or she is a winner. Notice that I said a winner—not the winner. Most people believe that in every negotiation someone wins and someone loses. That's sometimes the case, but in a successful negotiation nothing could be further from the truth. In fact, believing that there must be a winner and a loser can actually undermine your chance of conducting a successful negotiation.

To conduct a successful negotiation, you must be clear on what you want going in. You must also be diplomatic so that you can help drive the negotiation to a place where everyone wins.

Creating the Right Atmosphere

Successful negotiations are often the result of the atmosphere in which the negotiation takes place. By that I don't mean the physical environment in which the two sides negotiate (although the right environment can help put everyone at ease); I mean the personal and psychological atmosphere. I cannot emphasize enough the role that your interpersonal skills play in the negotiation process. Here are some essentials:

- Establish trust, credibility, and rapport
- Use the seller's name
- Learn the seller's interests
- Be an empathetic listener

Your first goal in any negotiation should be to establish trust and credibility with the other party. I once read that people are successful in life only to the degree that they are able to make people like them and trust them. This is certainly true in negotiating.

> "At least give it a try. What isn't tried won't work."
>
> ~Claude McDonald

When talking to a seller, take a few minutes to establish the rapport, or the trustful relationship, that is so essential to negotiating. If sellers feel comfortable with you, they often will be more forthcoming with important information, such as their true needs, than they might otherwise be.

If you are meeting the seller for the first time, learn the seller's name and use it over and over again in the conversation. Every person likes to hear his or her name said (in a friendly way), and doing so makes the other party feel valued and important.

Also, try to learn the seller's interests. If you are purchasing a single-family home, for example, look around the house when you visit the property. You might be able to discover some clues about the seller's interests, whether it is sports paraphernalia or a doll collection. Pick up on your observations and bring up these things in conversation.

As you talk to the seller, remember to always be an empathetic listener. Imagine yourself in his or her situation and try to experience, emotionally, what the seller is experiencing. By doing so you might gain a new perspective on the negotiation and be able to make an offer that the seller is likely to accept. Also, people like to know that they're being listened to, and doing so will help establish rapport.

> *"I've often found that it is the little things that cause negotiations to fail. Be courteous and try not to be offended or offend sellers to avoid negotiation roadblocks."*

Being Diplomatic

Diplomacy is critical to successful negotiations. Avoid overly criticizing the property, and never criticize the seller. Many people believe that by being overly critical they can actually force a seller into lowering the price or give more favorable terms. This couldn't be further from the truth. As a matter of fact, this tactic usually backfires and only makes the seller less flexible.

If you need to mention some of the property's weaknesses to the seller, do so in a nice way without being critical. You don't have to deliberately overlook the faults of a property. If the building has a flat roof, for example, you could ask, "Have you had any leakage problems with the roof? I've heard that flat roofs present some unique problems." Or, if the property is on a very busy street, you might say, "The property is really close to a busy street. It's pretty noisy, isn't it?" By pointing out some of the flaws in a nice way, you let the seller know that you are aware that the property is not perfect, yet you are being careful not to offend the seller. This conditioning may help the seller understand why your eventual offer (if you decide to make one) is well below the asking price.

notes:

Likewise, don't be timid about praising those aspects of the property that make it appealing to a buyer. This can work wonders in creating a positive emotional environment. Think about your own reaction if you were the seller. Most likely, you would want to work with someone who makes you feel good about yourself and your property. Someone who attacks your property might make you feel criticized, and you would automatically become defensive. Negotiations reflecting this mindset are likely to fail.

Evaluating the Needs of the Buyer and Seller

Whether you are purchasing a single-family home or an apartment building for $6 million, your negotiations are going to center around six variables:

- Price
- Terms (interest rate, amount, and length of mortgage)
- Down payment
- Closing date
- Monthly payment
- Personal property (for example, appliances) to be left with the property

When you begin negotiating you'll probably know your needs and wants— so you'll know what you want to achieve in the negotiation. It's quite easy, however, to overlook one of your most important needs—the seller's needs.

The more you can learn about a seller's needs, the more effective you will be in your negotiations. All that you generally know about the seller is what he or she wants—that is, the asking price and terms. Actually, such wants might or might not match the seller's needs, and he or she might not even be aware of the fact!

When you deal primarily with flexible sellers, becoming familiar with the reasons why a seller is flexible is important. In other words, find out what has made the seller flexible. Is it loss of employment, divorce, inheritance, job transfer, or management headaches? Or does the basement wall have an incurable leak?

When you ask the seller about his or her financial needs, the answers you hear will tell you the seller's wants. Usually the response is something like "I need all cash." Asking the seller how the cash will be used might be appropriate. If the seller responds by saying that the need relates to the purchase of another home, you might explain some creative financing techniques that would allow the seller to buy the home with no money down. If the seller responds with, "My reasons don't matter, I just need the cash," you might then say, "I would like to give you your cash down payment. But could we spread it out over a short period of time—say 48 or 60 months?" The seller might even respond by saying, "It is none of your business," in which case, you could respond, "I apologize for

notes:

asking. I just thought that by knowing the answer to that question, we might work out a way I could buy your property so that it would work out for both of us."

Developing a Negotiation Strategy

Before walking into a negotiation, you need to develop a strategy. If you don't have one, you won't know whether or not you're progressing toward your goal of a win/win negotiation. To determine your strategy, you need to establish your goals, your BATNA*, and your walk-away position (see next section). You also need to decide what you might use as nonessential contingencies to barter in the course of the negotiation.

Determining Your Goals, BATNA, and Walk-Away Position

If you ever take a course in negotiation (you should add that to the list of continuing education courses you'll want to take), you'll hear about the importance of BATNA. BATNA stands for "best alternative to a negotiated agreement." Basically, it means what you'll do if the negotiation fails. Determining your BATNA before going into a negotiation can give you a pretty good idea of how flexible you can afford to be.

Your walk-away position is your bottom line. If the seller asks for too much—or at least more than you're willing to give—and is unresponsive to any reasonable alternatives that you suggest, you'll need to get up from the negotiation table and walk away, regardless of how much time you've spent researching the property and putting together the deal. If you don't establish (to yourself) your walk-away position before you go into the negotiation, you might give in on some points and regret it later. Be sure to remember, when you do walk away, don't burn your bridges.

Using Nonessential Contingencies

Compromise is what negotiations are all about. If you enter negotiations with an open mind, the seller is more likely to have an open mind, too. This mindset allows both of you to create a win/win situation.

During negotiations both parties must give something to get something; therefore, good negotiators always use nonessential (but purposeful) contingencies as negotiating tools. In other words, when you use a nonessential contingency, you ask for concessions that you do not necessarily need or even want (concessions you are willing to "negotiate away"). In return, the seller concedes on a point that is important for you. For example, you might use one or more of the following nonessential contingencies:

*BATNA is a trademark of Eric C. Gould. Copyright©2000.

- The mortgage is to be amortized over 40 years instead of 30 years.

- The seller is to pay all closing costs instead of just part of the closing costs.

- The seller warranties all appliances for a period of one year following closing.

- The seller will repaint the interior and/or exterior of the property.

- The seller is to leave one or more pieces of furniture and/or window treatments.

By using nonessential contingencies, you will arm yourself with effective negotiating tactics. You might only want the seller to pay all of the closing costs, for example, but by adding the others, you have some extra items that you can give up to get the one that you truly want.

> *"Using diplomacy, once again, at the final negotiation table and re-establishing a rapport, if necessary, lets the seller know that this is a friendly transaction and that neither party is trying to take advantage of the other. Use the opportunity to reinforce your commitment to the idea that both you and the seller must work toward a win/win settlement."*

Educating the Seller

From time to time you will meet a seller who has some misunderstandings about how real estate deals work. It might be that the seller's knowledge (or presumed knowledge) is incorrect. If you argue or disagree with the seller, it doesn't matter who is right or wrong, you are going to lose in the negotiating process. If you appear to insult the seller's intelligence, you are going to create a negative negotiating environment.

If you must educate the seller, be very tactful. One of the best ways to do this is by telling third-party stories. For example, if the seller says something like, "The house down the street sold for $150,000. Mine is much nicer than that one," and you have already researched the neighborhood and know that the other house did not sell for $150,000, you might say, "I thought the other house sold for that amount, too. But when I was talking to a broker the other day, I found out that the house only sold for $135,000." You relieve tension when you explain or educate using third-party stories, and the seller does not feel like you are trying to cram something down his throat.

notes:

letter of intent —A letter stating a buyer's intent to make an offer to acquire a certain property. It is not a binding contract.

multiple offers —Usually conveyed through a letter of intent putting forth three or four different scenarios, any one of which would be an acceptable way to purchase a seller's property.

net offer —An offer in which the purchaser agrees to pay 100% of closing costs, thereby netting an amount to the seller that is the same as the seller's equity.

MAKING THE OFFER

At some point in time, you'll want to make an offer. There are various ways you can communicate your offer. You can make a verbal offer or write a *letter of intent*. You might also consider making *multiple offers* or a *net offer*.

Verbal Offers and Letters of Intent

One of the reasons people do not make more offers is that a carefully drafted written offer can take as much as an hour to complete. If the offer is declined by the seller, the buyer is made to feel that he or she has wasted the time spent trying to buy a particular property. Even though he or she might know that real estate is a numbers game, and that it is often not possible to have more than one offer accepted out of 10 or 20 made, it is still discouraging to spend a lot of time crafting a written offer only to have it rejected. Because of this, it might be appropriate for you to make verbal offers or use a letter of intent.

If you are looking at several properties, particularly those that are for sale by owner, you may want to verbally suggest to the seller that you would be willing to pay a certain price for the property or perhaps to obtain a lease option on it. You could then give the seller a business card and write on the back, "I would like to negotiate a lease option of approximately $150,000. Call me if you are interested."

You might even offer to give the seller a $10,000 down payment. The cash could come from a partner, a credit card, or be paid in installments by getting the seller to agree to take the $10,000 over 48 to 60 months (see Figure 13.1).

> *"The multiple offer can be a powerful tool when you are convinced that the seller will negotiate on terms or on price."*

If you're working with a real estate broker or agent, using verbal offers summarized on the back of business cards is inappropriate and not very productive. In cases like this, you should consider using a letter of intent. Letters of intent are not binding for either party but are indications of a good faith desire to own a property. If a seller responds in an affirmative way, it can be the basis for positive negotiations. If you are using a letter of intent on property that was shown to you by a broker, the letter of intent could be addressed to either the seller or the broker or agent.

notes: _____

Letter of Intent

100 Main Street
Anywhere, State
September 1, 2002

Ms. Jane Seller
123 Desire Street
Anywhere, State

123 Desire St.
Anywhere, State

Dear ___*Ms. Seller*___ ;

This letter is being written to express my sincere interest in purchasing your home located at 123 Main Street.

I am willing to purchase your home under either of the following scenarios:

I will pay you $150,000 with $10,000 cash down, to be paid over a reasonably short period of time. I would ask that you take back a $140,000 purchase money mortgage, amortized over 30 years but with a balloon at the end of 84 months. This mortgage would be payable monthly at a reasonable rate of interest.

OR

I will pay you $138,480 cash, with a closing to take place within 30 days.

Ms. Seller, if either offer is acceptable, I look forward to meeting with you to firm up the exact details of the closing and draw up a contract. At that time, I will give you an earnest money check in an amount acceptable to you.

Thanks in advance.
Cordially,
Joe Buyer

Figure 13.1: Example Letter of Intent

notes:

The whole point of the letter of intent is to try to arouse interest on the part of the seller and establish some common ground for negotiation. The great thing about letters of intent is that they can be written in a very short time, allowing you to write several letters during the period of time it would normally have taken you to write one contract.

Letters of intent can even incorporate the multiple-offer concept that we'll be talking about next. In effect, this allows you to present two or three different purchase scenarios on a property.

> *"Most people believe that negotiating is the process of determining a winner and a loser. Nothing could be further from the truth."*

Making a Multiple Offer

The multiple offer is a powerful tool when you are convinced the seller will negotiate on terms or on price. To make a multiple offer, you present several purchase scenarios that are acceptable to you. The theory is that when the seller has several choices, it's easier to accept one of them. Given only one offer, the seller might make a counteroffer or reject it completely.

When using the multiple offer concept, don't let the seller "cherry pick" the terms from each of the offers. You must tell the seller that each offer stands on its own as a package of price and terms that you think you can live with.

Proposing a Net Offer

In a net offer the seller gets a certain net amount of cash for the property. All of the costs of closing are paid by the buyer, including transfer taxes, recording fees, title insurance, real estate brokerage commissions, and inspections. The seller knows that whatever amount of money (or notes) that you offer, over and above any debt on the property, is the amount he or she will have when leaving the closing table. This offer strategy is best used to acquire lower or no equity properties.

For an example of a net offer, see Chapter 11, *Using Creative Financing Techniques,* Technique 11.

USING NEGOTIATION AND OFFER CHECKLISTS

No one can remember every aspect of negotiation tactics and strategies. So, to help you negotiate and make offers, I present the following checklist, which also includes some important principles of negotiation:

Preparing for the Negotiation

1. Don't fall in love with a piece of property. When this happens, you lose your objectivity and with it, your negotiating skills. However, if this does happen, don't let the seller know!

2. Deal primarily with flexible sellers whose properties have favorable existing financing.

3. Establish credibility and a friendly rapport with the seller.

4. Do not overly criticize the property and do not criticize the seller at all. Be diplomatic.

5. Do not use "fear" words. For example, instead of talking about a contract, talk about the paperwork.

"The more you can learn about a seller's needs as they relate to the sale of the property, the more favorable the negotiating outcome will be for you."

Conducting the Negotiation

1. Make sure all owners are present, if possible.

2. Use third-party stories to educate the seller.

3. Remember the power of simplicity. Don't act like you know everything, and don't be the first to mention price.

4. Don't ask for the moon. Ask for more than you expect to get, but imply that you're flexible.

5. You do not have to do all the talking. Be a good listener and after you make an important negotiating point, be quiet. The silence can be deafening.

6. Use nonessential contingencies.

notes:

7. Present your offer from the bottom up. (Bottom up means discussing contingencies and minor issues before you mention your offering price or major issues. Make sure you have lots of giveaways.)

8. Set aside issues that are deal busters.

9. Be sure your body language gives the same message that you are giving verbally.

10. If it appears that there can be no agreement, then leave the paperwork and give the seller the option to contact you by a certain time that day.

11. If tension develops, be calm and temporarily change the subject.

12. Remind the seller that peace of mind and mental relaxation will come once the property is sold.

13. When possible, explain the cause of your inflexibility. For example, explain that your attorney, spouse, or uncontrollable circumstance is the cause.

14. Make sure the seller has your name and phone number so that you can be contacted at a later date if the negotiation initially fails.

Making the Offer

1. Always make offers with uneven figures. For example, offer 8.7% interest instead of 9% or a price of $135,560 instead of $136,000. The seller might think you have a specific reason for doing so.

2. If you're offering a low interest rate, state it in dollars rather than as a percentage. Monthly interest of $50, or $150 per quarter, on a $10,000 mortgage sounds better than 6% interest.

3. Present your offers in person, not over the phone.

4. Make sure all final offers are in writing.

5. Consider using multiple offers and/or net offers.

6. Never give a seller more than 24 hours to accept an offer.

7. Win or walk, but don't be offensive.

notes:

REVIEW
Summary
Successful negotiation results in a win/win situation for both buyer and seller. It's very important to establish trust and credibility so you can keep the negotiations and offering processes as positive as possible. If you are diplomatic and remain objective about a property's faults, you can avoid the perception that you are criticizing the seller.

For successful negotiations, you must make sure you create the right negotiating atmosphere and be diplomatic. To prepare for the negotiation, you must evaluate the needs of all parties involved and develop a strategy that you will use to guide your actions. The strategy should include consideration of your goals, BATNA, and your walk-away position. When you conduct the negotiation, you should make sure to continually build rapport and trust with the seller. Sometimes it may also be necessary to educate the seller, using third-party stories, to make sure that he or she understands the transaction.

The initial offer can take different forms—for example, verbal offers, letters of intent, multiple offers, and net offers. All have advantages and disadvantages. You should become familiar with them to choose the one that best suits your needs.

Questions
• What are two basics of successful negotiation? (See page 13-1.)

• Why is it important to be diplomatic in negotiations? (See page 13-2.)

• What are the six variables of a real estate negotiation? (See page 13-3.)

• What is a walk-away position and why is it important in developing a negotiation strategy? (See page 13-4.)

• What is a nonessential contingency and how does it help you in a negotiation? (See page 13-4.)

• How can verbal offers help you in your investing efforts? (See page 13-6.)

• Why should you consider making a multiple offer? (See page 13-8.)

notes:

ACTION STEPS

The more prepared you are, the more likely you are to be a successful negotiator.

1. Contact three local real estate agents to determine if they know of any flexible sellers among their current listings or past transactions.

2. Assume you are a buyer and compile a list of nonessential contingencies on your own home or apartment.

3. Review the checklists presented in this chapter so that you are familiar with all aspects of the negotiation process.

FINAL COMMENTS

There's a lot of stress involved in selling properties, and a tremendous amount of peace of mind and relaxation once an agreement is reached. Successful negotiating is the key. Many people pay too much or sell for too little because they are uncomfortable with the negotiation process. If you learn how to negotiate, you will give yourself a big leg up when it comes to making deals. Remember, you must be persistent!

ADDITIONAL INFORMATION AND RESOURCES

Books to Read

- *You Can Negotiate Anything,* by Herb Cohen

- *Secrets of Power Negotiating,* by Roger Dawson

- *Getting to Yes,* by Roger Fisher and William Ury

NOTES

CONTRACT

*"The wealth of **knowledge** and **experience** obtained over years of investing was used to develop the **contracts** provided in this course for your use. They will lay the **foundation** for **successful transactions** for you, both as a buyer and as a seller."*

 Carleton Sheets

DRAWING UP THE CONTRACT

Because real estate transactions involve contracts, it is important to understand basic contract law and to know the various clauses that are included in a standard real estate contract. Such knowledge allows you to structure your contracts so that they benefit you—whether you are the buyer or the seller.

In this chapter, you will learn:

- How to use a real estate contract to your advantage.

- How to structure a real estate transaction that will be beneficial to you as a buyer or a seller.

When you complete this chapter, you will be able to:

- Understand the provisions contained in a real estate contract.

- Structure a real estate transaction to your advantage whether you're buying or selling a property.

My *Real Estate Forms Portfolio*, which you received with this course, contains many forms to facilitate the contract process, including:

- *Deposit Note* form, to be used when making the initial deposit.

- *Quit Claim Deed*, which could be used to transfer real property.

- *Attorney Approval* form, which grants each party the right to have an attorney examine the contract.

- *Closing Statement*, which reflects the contract payment provisions and all prorations.

More important, my *Real Estate Forms Portfolio* also includes two different versions of a real estate contract—one designed for you to use when you buy a property, and the other to be used when you sell a property. In this chapter, I outline the important provisions of each.

*(It is advised that any documents you use from this manual or the **Real Estate Forms Portfolio** be approved by a local attorney who knows your particular state's laws.)*

notes:

THE IMPORTANCE OF UNDERSTANDING THE CONTRACT

When you buy or sell property, the real estate contract that you use outlines the terms of the deal as agreed to by the parties involved. It's vital, therefore, that you familiarize yourself with each paragraph in the contract so that you can adjust the contract, as necessary, to meet your needs in any given real estate transaction.

I do not intend to make you a legal expert in the drafting of a contract. Rather, I want to provide you with the information, knowledge, and guidelines necessary for you to write your own contract, or to direct the person who is doing it for you. Based on the size of the transaction, the type of property, and the complexity of the agreement, it is ultimately your decision whether you write the contract or have someone else write it for you. Regardless of whether you use an attorney, a broker, or write the contract yourself, you need to be familiar with how a contract is put together.

BASIC CONTRACT LAW

A contract is really nothing more than a meeting of the minds—an agreement between two or more people to do or not to do a particular thing. While not all contracts are required to be in writing, real estate contracts, by law, must be written to be enforceable. When you make an offer on a property, that offer is neither binding nor does it constitute a contract until accepted by the other party. Once it is accepted in writing, both parties are bound, and neither can legally withdraw without facing the consequences of default. Before acceptance, the person making the offer can withdraw it at any time, even if they have a time limit for acceptance several days in the future.

The title insurance company or lawyer who handles the actual closing of the sale, uses your contract as a guide in preparing the deed to transfer title and any mortgages or leases involved. Therefore, the contract must accurately reflect the agreement between the buyer and the seller.

USING A REAL ESTATE CONTRACT

The real estate contract is a written document that outlines the terms of the deal you are making with the other party or parties involved in your real estate transaction. Although the entire contract covering the transaction can be hand-written, the large number of items that are covered in the agreement dictate that most contracts these days are preprinted. Unfortunately, most of the preprinted

> *"Decisions determine destiny."*
>
> –Frederick Speakman

notes:

boilerplate —The pre-printed routine terms and conditions of a contract.

Addendum (or rider) —An attachment to a real estate contract, signed by both parties, that spells out extra items and agreements not covered in the pre-printed contract.

portions of a standard real estate contract, known as the *boilerplate*, are written to benefit the seller rather than the purchaser. To help you, whether you're buying or selling, I have included two different real estate contracts in the *Real Estate Forms Portfolio*—the *Real Estate Purchase Contract*, to be used when you buy a property, and the *Real Estate Sales Contract*, to be used when you sell a property. Both contracts follow the same outline and paragraph numbering, but I have designed the wording of each one to benefit you, whether you're buying or selling.

Many times, specific agreements between the buyer and the seller are not covered in the boilerplate of the preprinted contract. When this happens, or when a buyer or seller finds it necessary to expand on the boilerplate information, one or both parties must add extra clauses or agreements to the contract. The clauses can literally be handwritten on the margins of the preprinted contract, but this is not a very professional way to conduct business. Typically, such extra items or agreements are included on a separate page known as an *Addendum* (or *rider*). The *Addendum* is dated and the names of the seller and the purchaser are added, as well as the contract date that the *Addendum* references. All of the details that are too numerous to spell out in the contract, and all of the essential and non-essential contingencies, are placed in the *Addendum*.

The contracts included in the *Real Estate Forms Portfolio* are legal in all 50 states. If you end up working with a broker or agent who is adamant about not using them, don't worry. Go ahead and let the broker or agent use his or her own contract. Just make certain that whatever portion of my preprinted contract you wish to use is included in the real estate broker or agent's contract as a part of the *Addendum*.

> *"The real estate contracts included in my Real Estate Forms Portfolio are excellent examples of contracts written to specifically benefit the buyer or seller—depending on which role you are taking. These contracts include many powerful clauses favoring and protecting you, whether you are buying or selling a property."*

Elements of a Real Estate Contract

Figure 14.1 shows an example of my *Real Estate Purchase Contract*, which you can use to make an offer on a property. You can use this contract in connection with the purchase of a single-family home, a mobile home, a multi-unit property, a commercial property, or even vacant land. I have titled it *Real Estate Purchase Contract*, but you should be aware that, in various parts of the country, it is also known as an Offer to Purchase, a Purchase/Sale Agreement, or an Escrow Agreement.

notes:

When you are initially making your offer to a seller, either directly or through a broker, always keep a copy of the offer for yourself. Later, when the seller has accepted the offer, or you have accepted the seller's counteroffer, make three copies of the contract. Give the original to the title company or lawyer, distribute copies to the seller and broker or agent (if one is involved), and keep one for your own files.

Notice that the very first line of the contract states, "WHEN COMPLETED AND SIGNED BY BOTH PARTIES, THIS IS A LEGALLY BINDING CONTRACT. IF THIS CONTRACT IS NOT FULLY UNDERSTOOD, THE SERVICES OF A COMPETENT PROFESSIONAL SHOULD BE SOUGHT." In other words, it's vital that you understand what a contract says before you sign it. So, with that in mind, let's examine each section of the *Real Estate Purchase Contract* shown in Figure 14.1 in detail. The contract sections are referenced either by their actual paragraph numbers or heading titles where no paragraph number is supplied in the actual contract.

REAL ESTATE PURCHASE CONTRACT

WHEN COMPLETED AND SIGNED BY BOTH PARTIES, THIS IS A LEGALLY BINDING CONTRACT. IF THIS CONTRACT IS NOT FULLY UNDERSTOOD, THE SERVICES OF A COMPETENT PROFESSIONAL SHOULD BE SOUGHT.

Seller, _____ , hereby agrees to sell to Buyer, _____ , or Buyer's nominee, the real property set forth below and all improvements thereon (herein referred to as the property), and Buyer agrees to purchase said property from the Seller on the terms and conditions set forth in this contract.

DESCRIPTION: The property is located in _____ County, (city/state) _____ and is commonly known as (address) _____ , has approximate lot dimensions of _____ x _____ , and is legally described as follows:

(If the legal description is not included at the time of execution, it may be attached to and incorporated herein afterward.)

1. PURCHASE PRICE: The total purchase price to be paid for the property by the Buyer is payable as follows:

(a) Earnest deposit .... $_____

(b) Sum due within _____ days after acceptance of this contract..................................... $_____

(c) Proceeds of new note and mortgage to be given by Buyer or any lender other than the Seller .... $_____

(d) Existing mortgage on the property which shall remain on the property but which shall not subject Buyer to any penalty or fee or increase in the original interest rate of said mortgage.................. $_____

(e) Balance due Seller by promissory note of the Buyer subject to the requirements set forth in this contract .... $_____

(f) Balance due Seller by Articles of Agreement for warranty deed.. $_____

(g) Additional sum due at closing (not including prorations) .... $_____

TOTAL PURCHASE PRICE.. $_____

2. APPORTIONMENT OF PURCHASE PRICE AND DEED: Land $_____ Building $_____ Personal Property $_____ . It is agreed that the property will be conveyed by recordable _____ warranty deed, with release of dower and homestead rights, subject to general real estate taxes for the current year, covenants, conditions, restrictions of record, and easements of record, all of which must be acceptable to Buyer.

3. BUYER will pay for recordation of deed and prorated share of prepaid insurance, taxes, and interest, if any.

4. THE SELLER WILL PAY FOR: [ ] Revenue stamps (state, county, and local); [ ] Title commitment in the amount of the purchase price from _____ or any title insurance company duly licensed to underwrite title insurance in the state of _____ ; [ ] Survey; [ ] _____ Attorney's fees; [ ] Appraisal fee; [ ] Real estate commission; [ ] Title abstract; [ ] Title opinion letter; [ ] FHA/VA mortgage discount; [ ] Photographs; [ ] Satisfaction of mortgage and recording fee; [ ] Lead-paint inspection; [ ] Home inspection; [ ] Repairs or replacements required by the FHA or VA not to exceed $_____ ; [ ] Any other inspections required by law. [ ] _____ .

5. ATTORNEY MODIFICATION: The terms of this contract, except the purchase price, closing date, and possession date, are subject to good faith modification (which may include additional terms) by the attorney for the parties within three (3) business days from the Contract Date (excluding Saturday, Sunday, and legal holidays). Notice of modification shall be in writing, served upon the other party or his agent, and shall state the specific terms to be modified and proposed revision. In the absence of written notice within the time specified herein, this provision shall be deemed waived by all parties hereto and this contract shall continue in full force and effect. The parties acknowledge that modification pursuant to this provision shall constitute a counteroffer.

6. PRORATED ITEMS: All rents, water taxes or charges, taxes, assessments, monthly mortgage insurance premiums, fuel, prepaid service contracts, and interest on existing mortgages shall be prorated as of the date of closing. If Buyer is to accept the property, subject to an existing mortgage requiring an escrow deposit for taxes, insurance, and/or other items, all escrow payments required to be made up to the time of closing shall be made to the escrow holder at Seller's expense and said escrow balance shall be assigned to the Buyer without compensation to the Seller; it being expressly understood that said escrow balance is included in the total purchase price. All mortgage payments required of Seller to be made shall be current as of the time of closing. If the exact amount of real estate taxes cannot be ascertained at the time of closing, Seller agrees to prorate said taxes on the basis of ___% of the last ascertainable amount.

7. TITLE AND TITLE INSURANCE: Within _____ days [ ] after the date of acceptance of this contract [ ] after the date of approval of Buyer's mortgage loan (if any), the Seller will provide and deliver to Buyer or Buyer's Attorney: [ ] A title commitment for an owner's title insurance policy in the amount of the purchase price (to be issued by _____); [ ] A title insurance commitment for a mortgage policy in the amount of $_____; [ ] A continuation of abstract.

8. SURVEY: Within _____ days [ ] after the date of acceptance of this contract [ ] after the date of approval of Buyer's mortgage loan (if any), the Seller will provide and deliver to Buyer or Buyer's Attorney: [ ] A new spotted certified survey having all corners staked and showing all improvements upon the property. [ ] No survey is required.

Seller _____

Buyer _____

Figure 14.1: *Real Estate Purchase Contract*, Page 1, Side 1

9. EXAMINATION OF TITLE AND TIME OF CLOSING: If the title evidence and survey as specified above disclose that Seller is vested with fee simple title to the property (subject only to the permitted exceptions set forth above acceptable to Buyer), this sale shall be closed and Buyer shall perform the agreements made in this contract, at the office of Buyer's Attorney, on or before [ ] _____ [ ] _____ days after the mortgage loan approval [ ] _____ days after acceptance of this contract. If title evidence or survey reveal any defect or condition which is not acceptable to Buyer, the Buyer shall, within fifteen (15) days, notify the Seller of such title defects and Seller agrees to use reasonable efforts to remedy such defects and shall have thirty (30) days to do so, in which case this sale shall be closed within ten (10) days after delivery of acceptable evidence to Buyer and Buyer's Attorney that such defects have been cured. Seller agrees to pay for and clear all delinquent taxes, liens, and other encumbrances, unless the parties otherwise agree. If Seller is unable to convey to Buyer a good and insurable title to the property, the Buyer shall have the right to demand all sums deposited by Buyer and held by or for the Seller. At the same time, Buyer shall return to Seller all items, if any, received from Seller, whereupon all rights and liabilities of the parties to this contract shall cease. However, the Buyer shall have the right to accept such title as Seller may be able to convey and to close this sale upon the other terms as set forth in this contract.

10. DEFAULT BY BUYER: If Buyer fails to perform the agreements of this contract within the time set forth herein, Seller may retain, as liquidated damages and not as a penalty, all of the earnest deposit specified in Paragraph 1(a), it being agreed that this is Seller's exclusive remedy.

11. DEFAULT BY SELLER: If Seller fails to perform any of the agreements of this contract, all deposits made by Buyer shall be returned to Buyer on demand, or the Buyer may bring suit against Seller for damages resulting from the breach of contract, or the Buyer may bring an action for specific performance. Buyer's remedies are cumulative and not exclusive of one another, and all other remedies shall be available in either law or equity to Buyer for Seller's breach hereof.

12. PERFORMANCE/DEFAULT/RELEASE OF EARNEST DEPOSIT: The earnest deposit and this contract shall be held by _____ (Escrowee) for the benefit of the parties hereto, and applied to the purchase price at closing.

13. CONDOMINIUM PROVISION: (a) If the subject property is a condominium unit, this contract is subject to the condition that Seller be able to obtain release or waiver of any right of first refusal or other preemptive rights of purchase created by the Declaration of Condominium within the time established by said Declaration. If, after making every reasonable effort, Seller is unable to obtain such release or waiver within the time provided and so notifies Buyer within that time, this contract shall become null and void and all of Buyer's deposits shall be returned to the Buyer, provided that if said option or preemptive right is not exercised within the time specified by the Declaration of Condominium, this contract shall remain in full force and effect for that period of time which the Declaration of Condominium provides for completion of the sale, should the option or preemptive right not be exercised. If the Declaration of Condominium contains no such option or preemptive right, this paragraph (a) shall be null and void and not part of this contract. (b) Seller represents and warrants that there are no condominium assessments currently due and owing. Seller agrees to pay any assessments, including special assessments, that have been or will be levied at any time prior to the date of closing.

14. ATTORNEY FEES AND COSTS: If any litigation is instituted with respect to enforcement of the terms of this contract, the prevailing party shall be entitled to recover all costs incurred, including, but not limited to, reasonable attorney's fees and court costs.

15. RISK OF LOSS OR DAMAGE: Risk of loss or damage to the property by any cause is retained by the Seller until closing.

16. CONDITION OF THE PROPERTY: Seller agrees to deliver the property to Buyer in its present condition, ordinary wear and tear excepted, and further certifies and represents that Seller knows of no latent defect in the property. All heating, cooling, plumbing, electrical, sanitary systems, and appliances shall be in good working order at the time of closing. Seller represents and warrants that the personal property conveyed with the premises shall be the same property inspected by Buyer and that no substitutions will be made without the Buyer's written consent. Buyer may also inspect or cause to be inspected the foundation, roof supports, or structural member of all improvements located upon the property. If any such system, appliance, roof, foundation, or structural member shall be found defective, Buyer shall notify Seller at or before closing and Seller shall thereupon remedy the defect forthwith at his/her sole expense (in which case the time for closing shall be reasonably extended as necessary). If the costs of such repairs shall exceed 5% of the total purchase price, Seller may elect not to make such repairs and the Buyer may elect to take the property in such defective condition and deduct 5% from the purchase price or Buyer may, at his/her option, elect to terminate this contract and receive the full refund of all deposits and other sums tendered hereunder. In addition, Seller agrees to remove all debris from the property by date of possession.

17. WELL AND SEPTIC TEST: (Select one applicable option)
[ ] The subject property is served by a community or municipal water and sewage treatment system (well and septic test provision inapplicable),
OR
[ ] The subject property is not served by a community or municipal water and/or sewage treatment system. Seller, at his expense, prior to closing, shall obtain and deliver to Buyer a water test performed by or acceptable to the county in which the property is located, a septic system test indicating that the system is in proper operating condition and in compliance with applicable state, county and local statutes, and have the septic tank pumped and emptied by a certified technician. Such tests shall be performed not more than 60 days prior to the closing date. If either of said written test reports indicate that the water is not potable, that the septic system is not in proper operating condition, or that the systems are not in compliance with the relevant statutes, Seller shall have the option to make the necessary repairs. If Seller fails to make the necessary repairs, then this contract, at the option of Buyer, shall become null and void, and all earnest money shall be refunded to Buyer.

Seller _____
Buyer _____

Figure 14.1: *Real Estate Purchase Contract*, Page 1, Side 2

18. FLOOD ZONE: Buyer shall have the option of declaring this contract null and void within 5 days of receipt of any written notice or disclosure, including the Residential Real Property Disclosure Report, that the property is located in a special flood plain hazard which requires the Buyer to obtain flood insurance. This option shall not exist in the event such written notice or disclosure was provided in a Residential Real Property Disclosure Report executed by both Seller and Buyer prior to the Contract Date.

19. OCCUPANCY: Seller shall deliver possession to Buyer no later than the closing date unless otherwise stated herein. Seller represents that there are no persons occupying the Property except the following tenants of the Seller:

_____

Seller agrees to deliver exclusive occupancy of the property to Buyer at the time of closing unless otherwise specifically stated herein. Seller agrees to provide true and accurate copies of all written leases to Buyer within five (5) days after the date of acceptance of this contract. Said leases are subject to Buyer's approval. Seller shall provide such letters notifying tenants to pay rent to the Buyer after closing as Buyer may reasonably request. Seller warrants that any rent rolls and other income and expense data provided to Buyer are complete and accurate, all of which must be acceptable to Buyer.

20. [ ] MORTGAGE OR THIRD-PARTY FINANCING: According to Paragraph 1(c) of this contract, it is agreed that Buyer will require a new mortgage loan to finance this purchase. The application for this mortgage will be made with a lender acceptable to Buyer, and unless a mortgage loan, acceptable to Buyer, is approved without contingencies other than those specified in this contract within _____ days from the date of acceptance of this contract, the Seller or Buyer shall have the right to terminate this contract and, at that time, all sums deposited by Buyer shall be returned to Buyer and Buyer shall return any surveys and copies of leases received from Seller. Notwithstanding the aforesaid provisions, if Buyer so requests and if Seller agrees, Seller shall have _____ days to offer Buyer a purchase money mortgage on said property at terms acceptable to and approved by Buyer, and this contract shall remain in full force and effect. Said purchase money mortgage shall be fully subject to the terms and conditions of the paragraph relating to Seller Financing below.

21. [ ] SELLER FINANCING: According to Paragraph 1(e), it is understood that the Buyer will execute and deliver at the closing, a promissory note to Seller which shall provide for full or partial prepayment without penalty [ ] and shall bear interest at the rate of _____% per annum beginning on _____ with payments in the amount of $_____ per _____ [ ] such that the amount of such payments shall amortize the debt due in _____ years with all unpaid principal and interest due _____ . The said promissory note shall be secured by a mortgage acceptable to Buyer and providing for the full and free right of the mortgagor to transfer the property, in whole or in part, subject to the mortgage and to substitute for the property other collateral of equivalent equity value; the exculpation of the mortgagor from personal liability; thirty (30) days' prior written notice to the mortgagor of the mortgagee's intention to commence foreclosure proceedings and the right of the mortgagor to cure; the subordination of mortgagee's lien to an existing or future senior encumbrance; the right of first refusal of the mortgagor if the mortgagee shall at any time sell its interest at a discount; future advances at the option of the mortgagee; the release of portions of the property from the lien of the mortgage upon partial principal payments by mortgagor, which said portion shall be released in the same proportion that the amount of the partial payment bears to the then outstanding principal balance.

22. [ ] ARTICLES OF AGREEMENT FOR WARRANTY DEED: If this sale is made by Articles of Agreement for warranty deed pursuant to Paragraph 1(f), then the terms of Paragraph 21 relating to Seller Financing shall be incorporated in said Articles of Agreement and shall become a part thereof, and the terms relating to a promissory note and mortgage shall be construed and relate to the Articles of Agreement for warranty deed in lieu of any reference to promissory note and mortgage.

23. FHA FINANCING: It is expressly agreed that, notwithstanding any other provisions of this contract, Buyer shall not be obligated to complete the purchase of the property described herein or to incur any penalty by forfeiture of any money deposit or otherwise unless the Seller has delivered to the Buyer a written statement issued by the Federal Housing Commissioner setting forth the appraised value of the property (excluding closing costs) of not less than $_____ which statement Seller agrees to deliver to the Buyer promptly after such appraised value statement is made available to Seller. The Buyer shall, however, have the privilege and option of proceeding with the consummation of this contract without regard to the amount of the appraised valuation made by the Federal Housing Commissioner.

24. VA FINANCING: It is expressly agreed that, notwithstanding any other provisions of this contract, the Buyer shall not incur any penalty by forfeiture of earnest money or otherwise be obligated to complete the purchase of the property described in this contract if the total purchase price exceeds the reasonable value of the property established by the Department of Veterans Affairs. The Buyer shall, however, have the privilege and option of completing this transaction without regard to the amount of reasonable value established by the Department of Veterans Affairs.

25. TERMITE INSPECTION: Seller agrees to furnish to Buyer, at Seller's expense, an inspection report showing all buildings on the property to be free and clear from visible infestation and free from visible dry or wet rot damage by termites and other wood-destroying organisms. This inspection report is to be furnished by a licensed pest control firm. If a report shows such visible infestation or damage, Seller shall pay all costs of treatment of such infestation and all costs of repair of such damage. If the costs of treatment and repair shall exceed 3% of the total sale price, Seller may elect not to make such treatment and repairs and Buyer may elect to take the property in its then condition and deduct 3% from the total purchase price and complete the transaction or Buyer may terminate this contract and receive a full refund of all deposits made by Buyer hereunder.

26. ZONING: Unless the property is properly zoned for _____ use and there are no deed restrictions against such use at the time of closing, the Buyer shall have the right to terminate this contract and receive a full refund of all deposits made by Buyer hereunder.

27. LEGAL USE: Seller represents and warrants to Buyer that the entire property conforms to all building codes and restrictions that may be imposed by any governmental agency either national, state, or local. Seller also warrants that there are no building code violations on the property and that Seller has received no notice of any building code violations for the past ten years that have not been fully corrected.

28. LOCAL ORDINANCES: Seller shall procure for Buyer, at Seller's expense, all certificates of inspection, certificates of occupancy, or the like required under the terms of any local ordinance.

Seller _____
Buyer _____

Figure 14.1: *Real Estate Purchase Contract,* **Page 2, Side 1**

29. PERSONAL PROPERTY INCLUDED IN THE PURCHASE PRICE: (Strike items not applicable): storm and screen doors and windows; awnings; outdoor television antenna; wall-to-wall, hallway, and stair carpeting; window shades and draperies and supporting fixtures; venetian blinds; window treatments; electric, plumbing, and other fixtures as installed; water softener; attached shelving; hardware; trees and shrubs; refrigerator(s) _____ ; stove(s) _____ ; air conditioner(s) _____ and such other items listed below or on a rider attached hereto, all of which personal property is unencumbered and owned by Seller. All such items shall be conveyed from Seller to Buyer by a Bill Of Sale.

30. THIS OFFER shall terminate if not accepted before (mo./day) _____ , (yr.)_____ .

31. RESPA COMPLIANCE: Seller and Buyer agree to make all disclosures and do all things necessary to comply with the provisions of the Real Estate Settlement Procedures Act of 1974 if it is applicable to this transaction.

32. ADDITIONAL TERMS AND CONDITIONS:

(a) Where the context requires, the terms that Seller and Buyer shall include are in the masculine as well as the feminine and the singular as well as the plural.

(b) There are no agreements, promises, or understandings between the parties except as specifically set forth in this contract. No alterations or changes shall be made to this contract unless the same are in writing and signed or initialed by the parties hereto.

(c) The provisions of this contract shall survive the closing and shall not merge in any deed of conveyance herein.

(d) This agreement shall be construed under the laws of the State of _____ .

(e) Other:

33. REAL ESTATE SALES COMMISSION: The Seller agrees to pay all real estate sales commissions due on this transaction.

34. NOTICES: Any notices required to be given herein shall be sent to the parties listed below at their respective addresses either by personal delivery or by certified mail - return receipt requested. Such notice shall be effective upon delivery or mailing.

TIME IS OF THE ESSENCE OF THIS AGREEMENT.

In witness whereof, the parties signed their names on the dates in the year set forth below.

Buyer(s): _____   Buyer's Date of Offer: (mo./day) _____ , (yr.) _____

_____   Address: _____

_____   Address: _____

Seller(s): _____   Seller's Date of Acceptance: (mo./day) _____ , (yr.) _____

_____   Address: _____

_____   Address: _____

Figure 14.1: *Real Estate Purchase Contract,* Page 2, Side 2

notes:

Seller and Buyer Information

This section should include the names of all of the sellers who have legal title to the property. If the seller is a corporation, the corporate name should be entered. If the title is held by husband and wife, it's appropriate to put "John and Mary Jones."

If you are the buyer of the property, enter your name in this section. Even though you might later transfer this contract to a partnership or other partners who may join you in the purchase, you are protected by the words, "Buyer's Nominee." These words would even allow you to sell the contract to someone else and make a profit before closing.

Description

This section includes the county and state in which the property exists. Where the form asks for the common description, "commonly known as," enter the street address. Generally you won't know the lot dimensions, so you can leave this blank. If you know the exact legal description, enter it here—for example, "Lot 4, Block 25, Timber Trails Subdivision." If you do not know the exact legal description write, "Exact legal description to follow."

1. Purchase Price

This section of the real estate contract describes, in detail, the terms and total purchase price for the property.

(a) Earnest Deposit

Enter any cash, check, or note you give to a real estate broker or seller. Sometimes, when I purchase property, I use a non-interest bearing promissory note that becomes due and payable at the time the transaction is closed. Once the offer is accepted, a seller sometimes asks for this promissory note to be converted to cash. If I agree to that, I will note it on this line. Regardless, the amount of that note is entered in the blank opposite the line following "Earnest Deposit," but is preceded by the words, "Promissory Note."

(b) Sum Due After Acceptance of the Contract

If I agree to pay an additional deposit after acceptance of the contract, which I generally do not do, it is noted on this line. The amount deposited varies. It could be zero or as much as 20% of the purchase price. The amount is open to negotiation and is usually an amount that convinces the seller that you are a serious purchaser. On the other hand, it is to the buyer's advantage to place as little money in jeopardy as possible. After all, the buyer loses the use of this money while the contract is pending and, even worse, could forfeit the deposit by failing to close the transaction. I try to keep my initial deposit to an amount less than $1,000, and do not like to have any monies due after acceptance of the contract. In that case, this line would be left blank. Depending upon the size of

notes:

the property you are buying, you may need to put down a deposit greater than $1,000. Brokers will often suggest that your deposit be at least 5% of the purchase price. However, this amount is totally negotiable, and I strongly recommend you try to keep this amount to a minimum.

(c) Proceeds of New Note and Mortgage From Any Lender Other Than Seller
On this line enter the amount of money that you are going to be receiving from any lender other than the seller. For example, enter the amount of money to be received from a bank or a private lender.

(d) Existing Mortgage on the Property
On this line enter the amount of any mortgage that exists on the property and that will remain after you purchase it. Even if you don't know the exact amount, enter an estimated figure.

(e) Balance Due Seller by Promissory Note
Any money that the seller is, in effect, loaning to you to buy their property is entered on this line. The loan is evidenced by either a note, or a note and a mortgage.

(f) Balance Due Seller by Articles of Agreement
You can also use this *Real Estate Purchase Contract* to buy property under an *Agreement for Deed*, also known as an Article of Agreement, Land Contract, or an Installment Contract. A separate form is not necessary. If you do choose to use this form to purchase a property under an *Agreement for Deed*, you should record this *Real Estate Purchase Contract* or an *Affidavit and Memorandum of Agreement*.

(g) Additional Sum Due at Closing
Any cash that you are going to give to the seller at the time of closing is written on this line. Note that this line does not include *proration credits*, which may substantially reduce this amount.

Total Purchase Price
Add all of the numbers that you have entered on lines (a) through (g), and enter the total purchase price you are paying for the property on this line.

2. Apportionment of Purchase Price and Deed
In this section you can break down the amount that you are paying for the land, the building, improvements, and any personal property. Depending on the age and condition, I will generally attribute approximately $1,500 to $3,000 of the purchase price for personal property in a typical single-family house. This apportionment of the purchase price can assist you greatly in maximizing your depreciation write-offs for the property. A word of caution, however—in some

proration credits —An amount credited at a real estate closing for any expenses that will be billed in the future (for example, sellers give a credit for their share of tax bills that will be billed in the future).

tax jurisdictions, personal property is taxed separately. Nevertheless, it is still possible to depreciate personal property separately for IRS purposes, even if it is not shown separately on the contract. The type of deed to be given by the seller is also noted. Usually, it is a general *warranty deed*, or general stamped warranty deed if there are transfer taxes due.

3. Buyer's Expenses

Here you note any expenses that you are paying in connection with the purchase. Usually I do not agree to pay for anything other than the items mentioned in this section.

4. Seller's Expenses

Almost every expense that's incurred in the purchase and sale of real estate is listed in this section. At the time you submit the contract, try to get the seller to pay for as many of these items as possible by putting a check mark in the box that precedes each item. You may want to refer to Table 15.2 in Chapter 15, *Closing the Transaction*, to see who customarily pays most of these costs.

Revenue Stamps and Other Transfer Taxes

All revenue stamps and transfer taxes are of taxes assessed against real property when it is sold. These taxes are imposed by local, state, and/or county governments. Usually the state or municipal statute provides which party is obligated to pay the tax. However, the buyer and seller can agree to pay for those items in any manner they like.

Title Commitment

This is a commitment for title insurance. Never buy a piece of property unless you obtain title insurance—and try to get the seller to pay for it. The seller usually pays for the insurance policy that covers the buyer. It is customary for the buyer to pay for the policy that covers his lender, as well as a fee to the title company for dispersing loan proceeds and processing the closing documents.

Survey

A current survey should be obtained prior to closing. In many instances, title companies will insure that the parcel is free of encroachments. However, it is best to have a survey in hand at closing. Most standard form contracts provide that the seller will provide a survey that is less than six months old. You should review the contract to confirm that this provision is included.

Attorney Fees

Attorney fees are for attorneys who work on the closing. Both parties usually pay their own respective attorneys fees.

warranty deed —A deed that conveys title that the seller warrants to be free and clear of liens and encumbrances (i.e., claims against the property).

notes:

Appraisal Fee
An appraisal is generally not required unless bank financing is being obtained. The cost of the appraisal is normally a buyer's charge that is likely paid before closing.

Real Estate Commission
The seller usually pays the real estate commission due on the transaction.

Title Abstract
An *abstract of title* is not required if you are obtaining title insurance. Title insurance is preferable to an abstract of title.

abstract of title —A summarized history of the title of real property listing rights and liabilities such as easements, mortgages, liens, and transfers of title. The abstract reports the status of the chain of title and whether or not the title is clear.

Title Opinion Letter
A title opinion letter is not required if you are obtaining title insurance. A title opinion letter is similar to an abstract of title. However, it is usually prepared by an attorney rather than a title company.

FHA/VA Mortgage Discount
This refers to discounts that are due in the form of points (one point equals 1% of the loan amount) if new FHA or VA financing is being obtained. Although this is a loan charge, usually paid by the buyer, the seller can assume responsibility to pay this charge.

> *"Time is of the essence—it is not discretionary."*

Photographs
Generally, photographs are not required. However, if an appraisal is ordered, the appraiser will take pictures and include them in the report.

satisfaction of mortgage — An instrument filed in the public records that acknowledges payment of an indebtedness secured by a mortgage.

Satisfaction of Mortgage and Recording Fee
If there is an existing mortgage on the property that will be paid off, the seller is responsible for making certain that a *satisfaction of mortgage* is recorded in the public records. You should also check to make sure it is recorded. Although this is a loan charge, usually paid by the buyer, the seller can assume responsibility to pay the charge.

Lead Paint Inspection
Most buyers don't request a lead-based paint inspection. However, it is a good idea to, at the very least, have the seller provide you with a completed disclosure. (I tell you more about this in Appendix B, *Environmental Issues.*)

Home Inspection
I always check this item, but I might not necessarily have a home inspected by a licensed engineer. Nonetheless, asking for a home inspection could assist you in your negotiations because you can use the home inspection as a giveaway item.

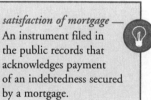

This is good example of what could be a nonessential contingency. The fee for the inspection may be paid by either the buyer or seller. It is a good idea to at least request that the seller pay for the inspection.

Repairs or Replacements Required by FHA or VA
This is necessary only if you are obtaining FHA or VA financing. If not, there may still be other repairs needed—so you could go to the next item, which happens to be a blank. Check it and write, "Repairs or replacements per attached Addendum." The seller is usually obligated to pay for repairs up to a set amount. If the seller refuses to make repairs beyond the set amount, the buyer has the option to withdraw from the contract or take on the responsibility to make the repairs.

Any Other Inspections Required by Law
Many municipalities have various occupancy requirements when a property changes hands. The seller is usually responsible for passing the inspection and paying any fees required to conduct the inspection.

5. Attorney Modification
This section affords both parties the opportunity to have the contract reviewed and accepted by their respective attorneys prior to being bound to the contract. However, purchase price, closing date, and possession date are terms that are not open to attorney review.

6. Prorated Items
This paragraph states that any charges, assessments, or expenses of any kind are to be prorated as of the date of the closing. If the closing takes place on January 31, the seller is responsible for 1/12th of all the costs of ownership on that property for the year. This paragraph also stipulates that all escrow balances—that is, the amount of money held by a third party for the payment of taxes and insurance—becomes the property of the buyer. Even if there is an overage in the account (more than enough needed to pay for expenses to the date of closing), the buyer still receives the entire balance. (This is truly a buyer's contract!)

7. Title and Title Insurance
Normally I give the seller 30 days after the acceptance date of the contract to deliver a title commitment for an owner's title insurance policy to me or my attorney. If I have a particular title company that I prefer doing business with (which I usually do), I write in the name of the title company in the blank. If not, then I will write in "To Be Determined."

8. Survey
If the seller is obligated to provide a survey, I generally allow 30 days from the acceptance date of the contract for this task to be performed. Generally, a

spotted survey is required. It is one that shows the boundaries of the property and also the location of all the improvements on the property. If no survey is required, then check the "No survey is required" box.

9. Examination of Title and Time of Closing

This paragraph directs that the closing will take place at the office of the buyer's attorney. If you do not have an attorney and are using a title company, cross off buyer's attorney and put in the name of your title company. You can then check the next box and put in the exact date you wish the closing to take place. If you are getting a new mortgage, check the next box and you might enter a date of 30 days after the mortgage loan approval. If you are trying to get the property rented before closing, you could put in the words, "See Addendum" instead of an exact date. Then, in the *Addendum*, note that the closing will take place when a tenant has been located or specify a closing no later than a certain date.

10. Default by Buyer

If you default on the contract—that is, you fail to perform according to the terms of this agreement, the seller's sole recourse against you will be the promissory note that you gave as an initial deposit of this contract. While I have never failed to go through with any real estate transaction for which I contracted, it is possible that a change in financial circumstances, death, or divorce could trigger a default. This paragraph limits your liability or that of your estate to the initial deposit paid.

11. Default by Seller

If the seller fails to perform, you may ask for a return of your deposit or, if you choose, take court action against the seller for *specific performance*. In other words, by filing a lawsuit you could ask the court to force the seller to sell to you.

12. Performance/Default/Release of Earnest Deposit

This section gives specific instructions for handling of the earnest deposit. It allows the parties to select a real estate broker, attorney, or escrow company to hold earnest deposits until closing. This section provides additional protection to the buyer against the loss of earnest due to seller dishonesty.

specific performance — A court order requiring a person to act or do a specific thing that he or she had agreed to.

13. Condominium Provision

This paragraph states that the seller must provide evidence from the condominium association that it is all right for the seller to sell the property. The condominium association must waive, in writing, any rights of first refusal, or other rights that it has against the unit. In addition, the condominium association indicates in this letter what past due association fees, if any, are outstanding, as well as outstanding liens, special assessments, or any other outstanding monies due. If you are not buying a condominium, cross out the entire paragraph.

notes:

14. Attorney Fees and Costs

This paragraph states that if any litigation results from this contract, the prevailing party (the one who wins) is entitled to recover all costs incurred, including attorney fees from the other party.

15. Risk of Loss or Damage

The seller is responsible for any loss or damage to the property up until the date of closing.

16. Condition of the Property

In this paragraph the seller agrees to deliver the property to the buyer in the condition it was in at the time the contract was signed. It further *warrants* that the seller knows of no defects in the property. Some states put the burden on the buyer to determine that there are, indeed, no defects of any kind on the property. Other states have statutes that require disclosure by the seller of any known defects. I strongly recommend that you request the disclosure report from the seller, prior to submitting an offer. If the seller is represented by a real estate broker, it is very likely that this report will be readily available. If not, you may have to get the disclosure form used in your state and have the seller complete it.

If there are any defects in the property, whether disclosed by the seller or determined by the buyer, the seller has the responsibility to repair such defects up to a cost of 5% of the total purchase price. If the seller does not make the repairs, the buyer may elect to take the property "as is" and deduct 5% from the purchase price as shown in the contract, or terminate the contract and receive a refund of all deposits. In the last sentence, the seller agrees to remove all debris from the property by date of possession. Since the word "debris" is somewhat nonspecific, I usually add, "and leave the property in broom-swept condition."

warrant —To guarantee something to be as represented.

> "*The Additional Terms and Conditions Paragraph 32, subsection c, provides that provisions of this contract shall 'survive the closing.' This is important to the buyer, because the seller may have made many warranties to the buyer within the contract.*"

Don't overlook this opportunity to have the property professionally inspected! Through the use of referrals, find an inspector who is extremely thorough. This is your opportunity to have all significant defects corrected by the seller, at the seller's expense. Otherwise, you will eventually be making these very repairs yourself at your own expense in the future. After the seller has made all the repairs and corrections, you should either inspect the repairs yourself or have the same professional inspector return to make sure all the repairs have been done correctly.

notes:

17. Well and Septic Test

This section requires the seller to disclose the source of the property's water and sewer system. If the property is not served by a municipality, the seller must provide a test ensuring that the system is in compliance and in good working condition.

18. Flood Zone

This allows a buyer to back out of a contract prior to closing within 5 days notice that the property is in a flood zone.

19. Occupancy

If there are any tenants on the property, their names are spelled out in this paragraph. If there are no tenants, then put the words "Not Applicable." Note that this paragraph also says that all "leases are subject to Buyer's approval." And the last sentence is very important. It requires that all of the income and expense data that the Seller provided to you must be "complete and accurate, all of which must be acceptable to Buyer." If you have previously obtained written income and expense data from the Seller (which you should always request), you can and should compare this data with the actual records and bills to make sure it is "completely accurate." I can tell you that sellers usually understate their expenses (and overstate their income), so this provides you with an opportunity to either void the contract or renegotiate the terms, if you so choose.

20. Mortgage or Third-Party Financing

If you are seeking outside financing and are not able to obtain the financing on terms that are acceptable to you, you can ask for a return of your deposit. Note that no specific interest rate or terms are mentioned, only terms that are "acceptable to Buyer."

21. Seller Financing

This paragraph is one of the most buyer-oriented clauses in the entire contract—and that's saying something! The seller agrees to subordinate his or her mortgage to another mortgage. If the seller is in first position at the time you buy the property, and you later choose to go out and get bank financing, the bank assumes a first position because the seller has already agreed, through this contract, to subordinate and assume a second position. It also states that:

- You can sell the property and let a new buyer assume the mortgage.
- You can substitute other collateral for the mortgage (another home or property in which you have the same or greater equity, for example).
- You will have no personal liability under the terms of the mortgage.
- You have a term of 30 days (instead of the normal 15 days) to cure a delinquency that you may have on the mortgage.
- You have a right of first refusal if the seller chooses to sell the mortgage at a discount.
- You have a *release clause* that allows you to release a portion of the property from the mortgage by a proportional payment. This is used in connection with an adjoining lot or vacant land.

release clause —A statement in a blanket mortgage that allows a specifically described parcel to be released from under the blanket lien after a sum of money is repaid.

notes:

There may be insufficient room in this paragraph to enumerate all of the terms and conditions of the mortgage the seller is taking back. If that is the case, in the small space below write these words, "See *Addendum* for exact terms. All other conditions within this paragraph apply." This is truly a powerful buyer-oriented paragraph.

22. Articles of Agreement for Warranty Deed

As stated earlier, if you are making an offer to purchase property under the terms of an *Agreement for Deed*, Land Contract, Installment Contract, or a Contract for Deed, this form may be used. All of the terms and conditions for seller financing as outlined in the previous paragraph apply. If you are not trying to buy a property under these terms, do not check this paragraph.

23. FHA Financing

If you are going to seek FHA financing to purchase a property, this paragraph applies. If not, cross it out.

24. VA Financing

If you are going to attempt to obtain VA financing in connection with the purchase, this paragraph applies. If not, cross out this paragraph.

Both paragraphs concerning FHA and VA financing stipulate that if the buyer is unsuccessful in obtaining financing through the FHA or VA, he or she has the right to complete the transaction using other alternative financing sources.

25. Termite Inspection

Whenever I buy property, I always require a termite inspection and, as you will note in this paragraph, the seller agrees to pay for it. If there is any damage, the seller is required to make the repairs up to 3% of the total sale price. If the repairs exceed that amount, the buyer still has the right to buy the property and, in lieu of the repairs being made, deduct 3% from the price as shown on the contract.

zoning —The laws that regulate and control how a property may be used.

26. Zoning

This paragraph is important for income property because the seller is warranting that the property is *zoned* for rental use. If you are purchasing a single-family home, put in the words, "Single-family residential rental." If you are buying a two-unit or three-unit property it is important that you put in, "two-unit or three-unit residential rental."

Notice that the seller states that there are no restrictions against such use. Other restrictions might include those that are made by a condominium board of directors that states that the property, cannot be rented to someone who is not on the title.

Also, in many parts of the Northeast, particularly New York, there are many so called mother/daughter properties. This is the name given to a home that has been converted into two living units, but not legally. They suggest that it would be appropriate for a mother and daughter; while this may be the case, the building is still not a legal two-unit property.

27. Legal Use
In this paragraph, the seller warrants that no building code, or other violations, exist for this property.

28. Local Ordinances
If required, the seller provides and pays for any certificates to show compliance with local ordinances.

29. Personal Property Included in the Purchase Price
This section lists a variety of personal property items that may or may not be included with the property. Go through the list and, if the items are not included, strike a line through them. If they are included, leave them as shown. If the list of personal property items is quite extensive and is greater than the items shown in this paragraph, you should spell out all of the personal property items in the *Addendum*. In that case, write in the words, "See *Addendum* for exact list." All items of personal property should be on a separate *bill of sale* at the time of closing. The deed does not transfer personal property.

bill of sale —A document used to transfer title to personal property (also known as chattel).

30. Time for Acceptance
On this line enter the time during which the seller may accept the offer. Generally, I do not give the seller more than 24 hours to accept an offer. If I am presenting an offer in the morning, I will frequently only give the seller until 6:00 p.m. of that day to accept the offer. As I mentioned earlier, an offer may be withdrawn any time before acceptance. If it is not withdrawn, and the seller does not accept it before the time stipulated on this line, the offer is automatically terminated.

31. RESPA Compliance
Since a title company or lawyer will probably be handling the closing, they will tell you and the seller what must be done to comply with the Real Estate Settlement Procedures Act (RESPA) of 1974.

32. Additional Terms and Conditions
Note that Paragraph 32(c) provides that this contract shall "survive the closing." This is important to the buyer because the seller has made many warranties to the buyer within this contract. In Paragraph 32(e), there is a space preceded by the word "other." If this space is adequate to enter all of the additional agreements between you and the seller, then an *Addendum* is not needed. Generally,

there is not enough room here, so most contracts do include an *Addendum.* Also, in any other part of the contract where you need more space, this is the area to use for the information.

33. Real Estate Sales Commission

If the seller is paying a real estate commission, it is noted in this section. If the buyer is paying the commission, it is included in the *Addendum.* If there is no real estate commission due, this section is crossed out.

34. Notices

This states how communication between the parties will be made.

Time Is of the Essence

This sentence states that all duties and obligations discussed in the contract must be completed by the date stipulated or the person not fulfilling their duties and responsibilities is in default. In other words, one minute late is not acceptable. Because of this sentence, if either party tried to contest performance that extended beyond the dates in the contract, very few judges or juries would rule in their favor. Time is of the essence; it is not discretionary.

Buyer's Signature Line

When you have filled out the contract in its entirety, sign the offer, date it, and put in your address. You should even add your telephone number. This way, if the seller refuses your offer, they have your address and telephone number, and you can be contacted at a later date.

Seller's Signature Line

If the seller accepts your offer as presented, the seller signs the contract and puts in the date of acceptance. If the seller wants to change any of the terms of the contract (i.e., make a "counteroffer"), they would still sign the contract, date it, and where changes are needed, make those changes right where they occur. For example, if the seller does not accept your purchase price but, rather, wants a higher figure, the seller puts in that figure next to your total purchase price offer and initials it. If you later agree to accept the seller's counteroffer, you put your initials next to their initials to show your acceptance.

HOW TO STRUCTURE YOUR TRANSACTION
Using My Purchase and Sales Contracts

A real estate contract can be structured so that it favors either the buyer or the seller. In the *Real Estate Forms Portfolio,* I have included two separate contracts for you to use. The *Real Estate Purchase Contract* favors you when you buy property, and the *Real Estate Sales Contract* favors you when you sell. Both contracts

notes:

contain all the elements described previously (see *Elements of a Real Estate Contract*), but there are important differences between them. It's very important, therefore, that you use the *Real Estate Purchase Contract* only when buying property and the *Real Estate Sales Contract* only when selling.

Example of a Real Estate Purchase Contract

As an example of using my *Real Estate Purchase Contract*, assume that you have found a single-family home on the market that you think will make a good rental property. The home is available for $150,000. You decide to offer the full price for the property, but you want to purchase the property with no down payment and a very nice cash flow.

The property has an assumable first mortgage with a balance of $69,800, which means that the owner's equity is $80,200 ($150,000 less $69,800 equals $80,200). The owner wants $25,000 in cash at the time of the closing and is willing to take the balance in the form of a note and mortgage at 10% interest, due in five years.

Based on your knowledge of the marketplace, you determine that $150,000 represents a fair market value and that you do not need an appraisal. (If you had determined that you needed an appraisal, you would have added that in the *Addendum* and made the contract contingent upon getting an appraised value equal to or greater than the price you are offering in the contract.)

A real estate broker has a listing on the property and has presented the property to you. The broker will earn a commission of $9,000 on the total selling price based on a commission rate of 6% (6% of $150,000 is $9,000.) The broker has consented to take a $9,000 note from you at the time of the closing. Because of this arrangement, you lower the offering price on the contract by $9,000 (the amount of commission you will be paying).

In Paragraph 33 of the contract change the wording to show that the buyer will pay the listing broker a commission of 6%. Then add the following statement after "Other" at the end of the Paragraph 32(e):

> • "Buyer agrees to pay broker a commission of $9,000, said amount to be evidenced by a promissory note bearing interest at 10% per year. The entire unpaid balance of the note shall be due and payable five years from the date of closing." (Note: Since 6% of $141,000 is $8,460, I will frequently negotiate with the broker to pay 6% commission based on the lower offer to the seller.)

You decide to offer a total of $150,000 for the property. Since you will be paying the 6% commission yourself, reduce the price by 6% so that the net price you are offering is $141,000:

- **On the front of the contract**—in Paragraph 1(a), write in your initial deposit as a non-interest bearing note in the amount of $1,000. This note is due and payable upon closing. Paragraph 1(b) is not applicable.

- In Paragraph 1(c)—next to "Proceeds of a new note and mortgage," write in $15,000. (Remember, the seller wanted $25,000 cash down payment, and was going to have to pay the $9,000 broker commission out of this, $25,000 less the $9,000 commission less the $1,000 promissory note due at closing equals $15,000.) Your intent is to sell a $20,000 second mortgage to an investor (third party) for $16,000 cash to be given to the seller. ($1,000 of this amount will pay off the promissory note due at closing.) Because you have agreed to pay the 6% brokerage commission, this $16,000 will provide the cash that the seller wanted.

- In Paragraph 1(d)—write in the principal balance of the existing first mortgage, which is $69,800.

- Next to the line in Paragraph 1(e)—that says, "Balance due Seller by promissory note of the Buyer," write $55,200.

When all of this is added together, the total purchase price will be $141,000. Once the amount of the broker's commission you will pay is added, the total you are offering for the property is $150,000. Your offer can be summarized as follows:

Item	Amount
First mortgage	$69,800
Proceeds from sale of new second mortgage (includes payoff of note)	16,000
Third mortgage taken back by seller	55,200
Note due to real estate broker (6% of original selling price)	9,000
Total price	$150,000

If you purchase a property with an existing mortgage and agree to assume the mortgage, you are agreeing to accept liability for it. By purchasing a property "subject to" the mortgage, you assume no liability.

After completing the balance of the contract, you are ready to begin work on the *Addendum*. It should read:

1. "Purchaser to take title subject to the existing first mortgage on the property. Any variation in the principal amount due from the amount shown on the contract shall be added to or subtracted from the note held by the seller." This is important! It protects you from having to come up with additional cash at closing should the mortgage balance, as presented to you, be incorrect.

2. "This contract is contingent upon purchaser being able to locate a buyer for a second mortgage in the amount of $16,000, said mortgage not to exceed a face amount of $20,000." (Note: When this wording is put into the offer, some sellers, realizing they can increase the selling price for their property—in this case by $4,000—will agree to accept the note themselves in lieu of cash.)

3. "Seller agrees to accept a third mortgage in the amount of $55,200, bearing interest and payable as follows:

   • Year 1—interest at 3%, with no interest deferrals.

   • Year 2—interest at 5%, payable 4% with 1% deferred, payments to be made monthly.

   • Years 3 through 6—interest at 5%, with no interest deferrals.

   " The deferred interest shall accumulate, but not compound, and the entire unpaid principal balance on the note, plus accrued interest, shall be due and payable six years from the date of the closing. Purchaser shall have no liability under the terms of this mortgage and the sole recourse of the seller shall be against the property encumbered herein, and not against the borrower personally."

4. "Seller agrees to turn over all escrow and utility company deposits to purchaser."

5. "Seller warrants that all appliances and equipment are in satisfactory working condition at the time of the closing."

6. "Buyer reserves the right to accompany broker to present offer."

Figure 14.2 shows how the *Addendum* for this purchase contract might look:

ADDENDUM

This Addendum is made the _3rd_ day of *(mo.)* _May_ , *(yr.)* _2004_ and is added to and amends that certain agreement by and between _Sally Seller_ as Seller(s) and _Billy Buyer_ as Buyer(s) which contract/agreement is dated the _3rd_ day of *(mo.)* _May_ , *(yr.)* _2004_ on the following property:

1234 Main Street, Hometown, New York

It is further agreed between the parties that:

1. Purchaser to take title subject to the existing first mortgage on the property. Any variation in the principal amount due from the amount shown on the contract shall be added to or subtracted from the note held by the seller.

2. This contract is contingent upon purchaser being able to locate a buyer for a second mortgage in the amount of $16,000, said mortgage not to exceed a face amount of $20,000.

3. Seller agrees to accept a third mortgage in the amount of $55,200, bearing interest and payable as follows:

   • Year 1—interest at 3%, with no interest deferrals
   • Year 2—interest at 5%, payable 4% with 1% deferred, payments to be made monthly
   • Years 3 through 6-interest at 5%, with no interest deferrals

   The deferred interest shall accumulate, but not compound, and the entire unpaid principal balance on the note, plus accrued interest, shall be due and payable six years from the date of the closing. Purchaser shall have no liability under the terms of this mortgage and the sole recourse of the seller shall be against the property encumbered herein, and not against the borrower personally.

4. Seller agrees to turn over all escrow and utility company deposits to purchaser.

5. Seller warrants that all appliances and equipment are in satisfactory working condition at the time of the closing.

6. Buyer reserves the right to accompany broker to present offer.

_____ Buyer(s)   _____ Seller(s)

_____ Buyer(s)   _____ Seller(s)

Figure 14.2: Example Real Estate Purchase Contract *Addendum*

notes:

PRESENTING THE OFFER

Hopefully, you will be able to accompany the broker when the offer is presented to establish some rapport with the seller, as well as to make certain that you communicate all of the benefits of the offer. After you arrive, ask to see the seller's home again. This will allow both you and the seller to become comfortable with each other. When the time is right, find a suitable place to talk to the seller about the offer. The kitchen table is a good location.

Present the offer from the bottom up, getting all of the nonessential contingencies out of the way first. Then talk about the seller's mortgage, and the income the seller will be receiving. For instance, in the example presented, you would explain that you are deferring a portion of the interest to allow you to almost break even on the property. Then discuss the second mortgage that you will be selling for $16,000 cash. You should also mention that you will be paying the brokerage commission yourself, so the seller will be getting only $16,000 cash (just what would have been netted if they had paid the commission), plus a note and mortgage in the amount of $55,200 to be paid off in six years. Finally, you would hand the seller a copy of your offer and say nothing else.

When You Sell—The Real Estate Sales Contract

Do not use my *Real Estate Purchase Contract* form when you sell property. It favors the buyer. Instead, use the *Real Estate Sales Contract*. Although very similar, it contains provisions that favor you, the seller. When you do go to sell a property, you should take the time to compare the two contracts. The two contracts look very similar, but there are important differences throughout. The provisions that favor the buyer in the *Real Estate Purchase Contract* have been changed or removed in the *Real Estate Sales Contract* to benefit and protect you when you are selling.

REVIEW
Summary

Understanding basic contract law and standard preprinted real estate contracts can give you an edge when you are ready to make an offer. To understand such contracts, you must study them and become familiar with their language.

To provide you with the contracts that you'll need for all your transactions, I have prepared two standard contracts, each of which is available in the *Real Estate Forms Portfolio,* as well as in electronic format in my *Real Estate ToolKit.*™ *The Real Estate Purchase Contract* is written to benefit you when you buy. *The Real Estate Sales Contract* is written to benefit you when you sell. You must understand the purpose of each section before you can structure a transaction to

notes:

your benefit. Any specific provisions not covered in the contracts should be included in an *Addendum*.

When you are ready to make the offer to a seller, start from the bottom up. Discuss the nonessential contingencies, then move on to the more important aspects of the contract before you actually present the written offer. When you finally present the offer, say nothing, and let the contract speak for itself.

Questions

- What is a contract? (See page 14-1.)

- What information might you include in an *Addendum*? (See page 14-2.)

- What is a creative way to make an earnest deposit when you are buying a property? (See page 14-8.)

- What are three of the items that are generally considered seller's expenses? (See page 14-10.)

- What is one of the most buyer-oriented clauses in the *Real Estate Purchase Contract*? (See page 14-15.)

ACTION STEPS

1. Make sure that you are familiar with all the important provisions that can help you make more profitable deals when you buy or sell property—study the details of the *Real Estate Purchase Contract* and *Real Estate Sales Contract*.

FINAL COMMENTS

Even if you decide that you are going to have a lawyer handle every one of your contracts, you still need to understand basic contract law and the implications of a contract.

NOTES

CLOSING

*"To be honest—I was extremely nervous at my first **closing**.
However, each subsequent closing was **less intimidating**.*

*After awhile, I understood that a closing was simply the
last step in the purchase **process** and there was nothing
to be feared.*

*In this chapter, I have described exactly what you **need to** do
to close on a property. **Follow my lead** and you'll soon realize that there is **no reason to feel intimidated**—even on
your first **closing**."*

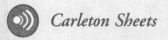 *Carleton Sheets*

CLOSING THE TRANSACTION

The real estate closing is the final meeting between the buyer and seller; where documents are delivered, closing papers are signed, expenses are apportioned, and the final adjustments to the transaction are made. To prepare for the closing, you must take care of certain details in the days and weeks leading up to the meeting. By carefully attending to these details, you will save yourself the aggravation that comes from participating in a closing where there can be unexpected and unfavorable surprises.

In this chapter, you will learn:

- Which documents guide the closing process.

- What you must do prior to the closing.

- What happens at the closing.

- How costs are allocated at the closing.

When you complete this chapter, you will be able to:

- Confidently and efficiently attend to all matters related to a real estate closing.

- Understand the figures presented on the closing statement.

- Know the satisfaction that goes along with a successful closing.

notes:

THE IMPORTANCE OF MANAGING THE DETAILS

Once your offer is accepted, you will probably have to meet certain contingencies and perform certain duties prior to closing the transaction. The first time you prepare for a closing, you might find yourself overwhelmed by the experience—it seems like there are so many details to address! Don't worry. If you attend to them calmly and thoroughly, using this chapter as your guide, you'll come through with flying colors.

With each property you purchase after the first one, you will find yourself feeling more and more comfortable with preparations for the closing. It's important, however, that you always refer back to the checklists in this chapter regardless of the type of property you're buying. Even the most experienced investor can sometimes inadvertently forget an important task.

PREPARING FOR THE CLOSING

Your general preparations, if any, for the closing should begin immediately upon acceptance of your offer. By getting a jump on preparations, you help ensure that your financing, if any, is approved in advance of the closing date, and that the lawyer or title company has enough time to complete preclosing tasks.

To properly handle the closing, you need to be familiar with the documents that guide the closing process. You must also know which tasks need to be performed prior to the closing itself.

Understanding the Main Closing Documents
There are four main documents that guide the closing process:

- Loan commitment/agreement
- Sales contract
- Title insurance commitment
- Closing statement

While the title company or attorney handling the closing will calculate all the costs and credits in advance of the closing, it is still important for you to understand the provisions of each document. This is advisable if only to check the accuracy of the calculations. In approximately 25% of the closings I am involved with, I find errors on the closing statement.

Documents Relating to Financing (loan commitment/agreement)
Unless you are paying all cash out of your pocket for the property, you will have

some documents relating to the financing. In most cases, the financing you obtain will fall into one or more of the following categories:

- Origination of a new mortgage loan
- Assumption of an existing mortgage
- Origination of a loan through some other source—for example, partners, family, the seller, equity loans, or credit card advances

Regardless of the type of financing you obtain, you must make certain that you understand the terms of your loan and the conditions required by your *mortgagee*. The terms and conditions should be laid out in a commitment letter or loan agreement. The terms of the commitment or agreement disclose such things as your loan amount, interest rate, payment term, upfront fees, and prepayment penalties, if any. This information allows you to estimate what funds, if any, you will need to bring to the closing and to assess the overall feasibility of the transaction.

> *mortgagee* —A lender of money under the terms of a mortgage.

The conditions of the commitment or agreement advise you of what you must do in order to obtain loan funding. Examples of common conditions include these: paying off existing debt, providing funds for closing, obtaining an appraisal, securing insurance, and clearing title. Many times, loan agreements or commitments are made to a buyer in advance of finding a property. This saves a lot of time once you find a property that you want to purchase, and it's a powerful negotiating tool as well. When a seller knows that you are pre-approved, they frequently will be more willing to negotiate. Conditions obviously cannot be addressed until you agree to purchase a specific property.

You should always review the terms of the loan to make certain that you understand what the loan will cost you—both upfront and throughout the life of the loan. (Even if your loan agreement is an informal one, such as with a family member, it's a good idea to have a promissory note that will include the important terms—for example, the loan amount, interest rate, and term.) You should also make certain to "clear" all conditions prior to closing. Some conditions might not be within your control, but you should follow up with the person responsible for each condition to ensure that it has been cleared. For example, if the seller's attorney is required to clear the title, you should check with him or her prior to closing to confirm that there are no problems.

Contract

The real estate contract is a written document that outlines the terms of the real estate transaction you are making with the other party or parties. It contains many items that are time-sensitive and require action prior to a specific date. Failure to act on one or more provisions can greatly affect your rights under the contract. Aside from performance dates, a contract typically contains time-sensitive contingencies. Table 15.1 shows some common contract performance dates and contingencies:

Table 15.1: Contract Performance: Contingencies and Consequences of Failure to Act

Contingency	Description	Consequences of Failure to Act
Finance contingency	Financing must be obtained or the seller must be notified that financing could not be obtained.	Failure to notify the seller that financing could not be obtained might result in the forfeiture of *earnest money*.
Additional earnest deposits	Additional earnest money must be paid.	Failure to pay might result in the forfeiture of the contract and any earnest money already deposited.
Termite inspection	Property must be inspected for insect infestation.	Failure to inspect might result in the loss of your right to cancel because of insect infestation as a reason to void the contract.
Lead paint inspection	Property must be inspected for lead paint.	Failure to inspect might result in the loss of your right to cancel because of lead paint as a reason to void the contract.
Home inspection	Property must be inspected for defects.	Failure to inspect may result in the loss of your right to cancel because of property defects as a reason to void the contract.
Rent rolls/lease review	Rent rolls and leases must be reviewed.	Failure to review might result in the loss of your right to cancel because of rent rolls and leases as a reason to void the contract.
Survey review	Survey must be reviewed.	Failure to review might result in the loss of your right to cancel because of survey as a reason to void the contract.
Owner's tax return review	Owner's tax returns must be reviewed.	Failure to review might result in the loss of your right to cancel because of owner's tax returns as a reason to void the contract.

earnest money —A deposit of money given by a party to bind the contract, usually credited toward the sales price.

notes:

Contingency	Description	Consequences of Failure to Act
Unit inspection	All units in a multi-unit property must be inspected.	Failure to inspect might result in the loss of your right to cancel because of the condition of any unit as a reason to void the contract.
Current expense item review	Current expenses must be reviewed.	Failure to review might result in the loss of your right to cancel because of current expenses (for example, real estate taxes, utility bills, or insurance bills) as a reason to void the contract.
Expense receipt review	Expense receipts must be reviewed.	Failure to review might result in the loss of your right to cancel because of expense receipts as a reason to void the contract.
Closing	Transaction must close.	Failure to close in a timely manner or have the closing date extended by mutual agreement might result in forfeiture of the contract and earnest money.

When you draw up the contract, you should put each performance and contingency date on your calendar and make certain you take the appropriate action in a timely manner. In addition to fulfilling the date requirements of your contract, you might need to make amendments to the contract after the initial signing. To avoid misunderstandings at closing, both the seller and buyer should sign any changes agreed to after the initial signing. Examples of common amendments include these: extended finance contingency dates, changed closing dates, added owner signatures, and purchase price changes.

The contract will also provide for documents that will be exchanged at or prior to closing. Documents you might need to follow up on or have prepared include the following: the title insurance commitment, association letter (if a condominium), insurance, notes, mortgages, bill of sale, deed, closing statement, and transfer declarations.

Title Insurance Commitment
The title insurance commitment is a report from a title company that discloses a property's *owners of record*, liens recorded against the property, real estate taxes due and paid, and all the documents required to ensure that clear title is being conveyed. Additional documents a title company might require include deeds,

 owners of record —All owners that are listed on a deed that is recorded in the county courthouse.

completed transfer forms, lien waivers, payoffs, releases, water bills, and proof of identification of the buyer and seller. A careful reading of the title report by the title company or closing attorney will identify the items needed, if any, to clear title before closing.

In addition to a search of the property records, title companies also search court records to determine if the seller or buyer has any outstanding judgments against them. If a judgment is discovered against someone with a name identical or similar to that of the buyer or seller, it might require the affected party to demonstrate that he or she is not, in fact, liable for the judgment.

In many cases, the seller or the seller's attorney will order the title and prepare and obtain the documents needed to clear the title. However, you should be capable of reading and understanding the title report. In particular, you should learn to recognize potential title issues such as sold tax certificates, pending bankruptcy cases, or code violation cases—any or all of which might indicate that the seller will have difficulty clearing title. At the closing, you should also confirm that the legal description on the title insurance commitment, deed, and survey are all identical. This way you can guard against receiving title to the wrong property. By following up to make certain that the title issues will be cleared, you can avoid closing-day disappointments.

Closing Statement

The closing statement lists the closing costs for all parties involved in the transaction. (To ensure that there are no unpleasant surprises, you should at least approximate costs, before making the offer.)

Whether you close the transaction at an attorney's office, a title company, or other closing agency, they will likely provide you with a *HUD1 RESPA Settlement Statement* (see Figure 15.1). This statement is required by the federal government and discloses the fees, costs, and charges associated with the transaction.

On the first page of the statement, the buyer's and seller's charges are listed in the left and right columns, respectively, and the columns are divided into upper and lower sections. The upper section of the buyer's column contains charges such as the purchase price and prepaid items; the lower section contains credits such as the loan amount and tax credits. The credits are deducted from the charges to compute the amount due at closing or the refund owed to the buyer. The upper section of the seller's column contains the seller's credits, and the lower section contains the seller's costs. The bottom line shows the proceeds to the seller or the amount due from the seller.

Failure to disclose fees, charges, and credits on this statement can constitute a violation of federal law. Accordingly, in any transaction requiring a *HUD1 RESPA* statement, you should make certain that the details of the transaction are accurately presented. If you are uncertain about any issue, don't hesitate to ask or seek legal advice.

OMB No 2502-0265   Computer form published by LAW DISKS, 734 Franklin Av, Garden City NY 11530 ~ 516-741-5740

A. U.S. DEPARTMENT OF HOUSING AND URBAN DEVELOPMENT HUD-1 UNIFORM SETTLEMENT STATEMENT

B. TYPE OF LOAN:	6. File Number	7. Loan Number
[X] Conventional-Uninsured		
	8. Mortgage Insurance Case Number	

C.   Note: this form is furnished to give you a statement of actual settlement costs. Amounts paid to and by the settlement agent are shown. Items marked "(P.O.C.)" were paid outside the closing. They are shown here for informational purposes and are not included in the totals. Note: TIN = Taxpayer's Identification Number.

D. Name and address of borrower	E. Name, address and TIN of seller	F. Name and address of lender
G. Property Location	H. Settlement Agent: name, address and TIN	
	Place of Settlement Office of Settlement Agent, above	I. Settlement Date:

J. SUMMARY OF BORROWER'S TRANSACTION		K. SUMMARY OF SELLER'S TRANSACTION	
100 GROSS AMOUNT DUE FROM BORROWER:		**400 GROSS AMOUNT DUE TO SELLER:**	
101 Contract sales price		401 Contract sales price	
102 Personal property		402 Personal property	
103 Borrower settlement charges (line 1400)		403	
104		404	
105		405	
Adjustments for items paid by seller in advance		*Adjustments for items paid by seller in advance*	
106 City/town taxes		406 City/town taxes	
107 County taxes		407 County taxes	
108 Assessments		408 Assessments	
109		409	
110		410	
111		411	
112		412	
120 **GROSS AMOUNT DUE FROM BORROWER**		420 **GROSS AMOUNT DUE TO SELLER**	
200 AMOUNTS PAID BY OR ON BEHALF OF BORROWER:		**500 REDUCTIONS IN AMOUNT DUE TO SELLER**	
201 Deposit or earnest money		501 Excess deposit (see instructions)	
202 Principal amount of new loan(s)		502 Settlement charges to seller (line 1400)	
203 Existing loan(s) taken subject to		503 Existing loan(s) taken subject to	
204		504 Payoff of first mortgage loan	
205		505 Payoff of second mortgage loan	
206		506	
207		507	
208		508	
209		509	
Adjustments for items unpaid by seller		*Adjustments for items unpaid by seller*	
210 City/town taxes		510 City/town taxes	
211 County taxes		511 County taxes	
212 Assessments		512 Assessments	
213		513	
214		514	
215		515	
216		516	
217		517	
218		518	
219		519	
220 **TOTAL PAID BY/FOR BORROWER**		520 **TOTAL REDUCTION IN AMOUNT DUE SELLER**	
300 CASH AT SETTLEMENT FROM/TO BORROWER		**600 CASH AT SETTLEMENT TO/FROM SELLER**	
301 Gross amt due from borrower (Ln 120)		601 Gross amt due to seller (Ln 420)	
302 Less amt paid by/for borrower (Ln 220)		602 Less reduction in amt due seller (520)	
303 CASH [X] FROM BORROWER		**603 CASH [X] TO SELLER**	

_____(Seller's signatures)_____

Figure 15.1(a): *HUD1 RESPA Settlement Statement*, Side 1

L. SETTLEMENT CHARGES	PAID FROM BORROWER'S FUNDS AT SETTLEMENT	PAID FROM SELLER'S FUNDS AT SETTLEMENT
700 **TOTAL SALES/BROKER'S COMMISSION based on price $ @ % =**		
Division of Commission (line 700) as follows:		
701 $ to		
702 $ to		
703 Commission paid at settlement		
704		
800 **ITEMS PAYABLE IN CONNECTION WITH LOAN**		
801 Loan Origination fee %		
802 Loan Discount %		
803 Appraisal Fee to		
804 Credit Report to		
805 Lender's Inspection Fee		
806 Mortgage Insurance Application Fee to		
807 Assumption Fee		
808		
809		
810		
811		
900 **ITEMS REQUIRED BY LENDER TO BE PAID IN ADVANCE**		
901 Interest from to @ $ /day		
902 Mortgage Insurance Premium for months to		
903 Hazard Insurance Premium for years to		
904 years to		
905		
1000 **RESERVES DEPOSITED WITH LENDER**		
1001 Hazard insurance months @ $ per month		
1002 Mortgage insurance premium for months @ $ per month		
1003 City property taxes months @ $ per month		
1004 County property taxes months @ $ per month		
1005 Annual assessments months @ $ per month		
1006 months @ $ per month		
1007 months @ $ per month		
1008 Aggregate Accounting Adjustment		
1100 **TITLE CHARGES**		
1101 Settlement or closing fee to		
1102 Abstract or title search to		
1103 Title examination to		
1104 Title insurance binder to		
1105 Document preparation to		
1106 Notary fees to		
1107 Attorney's fees to		
(includes above item numbers)		
1108 Title insurance to		
(includes above item numbers)		
1109 Lender's coverage $		
1110 Owner's coverage $		
1111		
1112		
1113		
1200 **GOVERNMENT RECORDING AND TRANSFER CHARGES**		
1201 Recording fees: Deed $ Mortgage $ Releases $		
1202 City/cty tax/stamps: Deed $ Mortgage $		
1203 State tax/stamps Deed $ Mortgage $		
1204		
1205		
1300 **ADDITIONAL SETTLEMENT CHARGES**		
1301 Survey to		
1302 Pest inspection to		
1303		
1304		
1305		
1400 **TOTAL SETTLEMENT CHARGES** (enter on lines 103, Section J and 502, Section K)		

CERTIFICATION: I have carefully reviewed the HUD-1 Settlement Statement and to the best of my knowledge and belief, it is a true and accurate statement of all receipts and disbursements made on my account or by me in this transaction. I further certify that I have received a copy of the HUD-1 Settlement Statement.

_____ Borrower   _____ Seller

_____ Borrower   _____ Seller

To the best of my knowledge the HUD-1 Settlement Statement which I have prepared is a true and accurate account of the funds which were received and have been or will be disbursed by the undersigned as part of the settlement of this transaction.

_____ Settlement Agent   _____ Date

WARNING: It is a crime to knowingly make false statements to the United States on this or any other similar form. Penalties upon conviction can include a fine and imprisonment. For details see Title 18 U.S. Code Section 1001 and Section 1010.

Figure 15.1(b): *HUD1 RESPA Settlement Statement*, Side 2

notes:

Using Closing Checklists

I have created three supplemental checklists—things to do immediately once your offer is accepted, things to do one week before closing, and things to do the day before closing. These checklists will guide you through the preclosing time period and you can refer to them as needed.

Things to Do Immediately

As soon as your offer is accepted, you should start taking care of details regarding financing and the real estate contract.

> *"Don't worry if you find yourself overwhelmed by your first experience closing a transaction. If you attend to the details calmly and thoroughly, using this chapter as your guide, you'll come through with flying colors."*

Financing

1. For existing financing, obtain permission to assume the mortgage.
2. For new financing, apply to at least two lenders. A lender that has access to many different mortgage programs is available at *www.CarletonSheets.com.*
3. For other money sources—for example, partners, family, equity loans, and credit card advances—begin to pursue your leads.

Contract

1. Insert the full legal description of the property into the contract.
2. Review the contract for performance dates. List all contingencies that must be met and the tasks that must be performed, with their completion deadlines—for example:

   • Additional earnest money deposits due.

   • Termite inspection.

   • Lead paint inspection.

   • Home inspection.

   • Rent rolls and leases, if any.

   • Survey, if required.

   • Review of owner's tax returns, if income property.

   • Inspection of every unit, if a multi-unit property.

   • Review of current expense items—for example, the most current real estate tax bill, utility bills, and insurance bills.

   • Verification of expense receipts.

3. Make sure that all owners of record—that is, all owners listed on the deed recorded in the county courthouse—have signed the contract.

4. Make copies of the contract to distribute to all interested parties—for example, the seller, broker, lawyer, and title company.

5. Present a copy of the contract to the title company or lawyer, who will:

   • Search the title for any liens or other matters of record that could affect your purchase of the property.

   • Calculate prorations.

   • Obtain required letters of approval from condominium associations.

   • Obtain *payoff letters* from lenders.

   • Issue the title insurance commitment.

   • Prepare any new notes, mortgages, and amortization schedules.

   • Prepare a bill of sale for personal property.

   • Prepare the deed or agreement for deed.

   • Prepare a closing statement of money owed by you (or payable to you) and money due (or from) the seller.

   • Handle the recording of all documents after the closing.

   • Mail copies of all recorded documents to all parties after the closing.

> *payoff letter*—A letter stipulating the exact unpaid balance, including interest through the date of closing, as of a given date (also called an estoppel letter).

Things to Do the Week Before Closing

In the week leading up to the closing date, you should attend to details regarding insurance, title, taxes, utilities, and renters (for a rental property):

1. Order insurance for the property.
2. Review the title insurance commitment to make sure the title is clear.
3. Obtain and review the closing statement (at least three days before closing).
4. Notify utilities, cable TV, and other service *vendors* of change in ownership.
5. Pay any local transfer tax, if it is your responsibility as the buyer. This charge may be paid from the proceeds of closing by the closing agent and will appear on the closing statement.
6. For rental properties:

   • Prepare a letter to tenants announcing the change in ownership. (These letter should be mailed immediately after closing.)

   • Run a newspaper ad for tenants (if vacancies exist).

> *vendor*—A seller of goods or services.

notes:

Things to Do the Day Before Closing

On the day before closing, you should inspect the property again and obtain the funds or other consideration you'll need to buy the property at the closing:

1. Thoroughly check the property—for example, all appliances, air conditioning, furnace, and plumbing—even if you had a home inspection done earlier.
2. Obtain a certified check for the funds required at closing. This will probably be made payable to the closing agent's escrow account.

> *"If you have the opportunity, so as to avoid potential conflicts and to expedite the transaction, you should consider going to the closing at a different time than the seller."*

HANDLING THE CLOSING

When you have completed all your preclosing tasks, and the inspections stipulated in the contract have been made, your final task is to close the transaction. You should also be aware that different regions of the country conduct closings differently. In some regions, the closing documents and funds are deposited with the title company, which then processes the deposited items and closes the transaction without the presence of the buyer and seller. In other regions, the buyer and seller attend the closing together and all matters are resolved on the day of closing. If you have the opportunity, so as to avoid potential conflicts and to expedite the transaction, you should consider going to the closing at a different time than the seller. You could even sign the paperwork at a different location than the formal closing. Being familiar with the method employed in your region will help you to become more comfortable with the closing process. If you have the opportunity at the closing itself, you will:

- Sign all paperwork.
- Deliver the certified check to the lawyer or title company officer.
- Obtain the keys and garage door opener.
- Obtain any warranties and maintenance and service contracts still in effect.
- Obtain the original copies of the leases if the property is rented.

With regard to costs paid at closing, the contract usually stipulates which party pays which item and whether the real estate taxes are prorated (and on what basis). In a typical real estate transaction, the costs of ownership and title transfer are usually allocated as shown in Table 15.2.

notes:

Table 15.2: Typical Allocation of Ownership and Title Transfer Costs

Item	Buyer	Seller	Comments
Real estate taxes	X	X	Prorated
Utilities	X	X	Prorated
Insurance	X	X	Prorated
Transfer tax	X	X	Per statute or agreement
Real estate agent fee		X	

Recording fees:
   New deed
   Old mortgage release
	X	X	

Survey	X	X	Per agreement
Lawyer fees	X	X	Each his or her own
Title fees	X	X	Each his or her own
Title Insurance	X	X	Per agreement

"Whenever you see a successful business, someone once made a courageous decision."

~Peter Drucker

Allocation of closing expenses are mainly determined by statute, contract terms, and local tradition—which can vary widely according to the region of the country in which the closing takes place. However, remember that everything is negotiable. (In a net transaction, as discussed in Technique #11 of Chapter 11, *Using Creative Financing Techniques*, you might end up paying all of these expenses. Conversely, you may negotiate a transaction in which the seller pays all or most of these costs.) Traditions used in Chicago, Illinois, for example, are not necessarily the same as those used in Seattle, Washington.

REVIEW
Summary
Once your offer is accepted, you must attend to certain details in order to prepare for the closing. General preparations, which include financing and contract issues, should begin immediately after the offer is accepted to allow time for completion prior to closing. In the week leading up to the closing, you should take care of matters concerning insurance for the property, the title insurance commitment, the closing statement, the transfer of utilities, transfer taxes, and notification of tenants

notes:

(for rental properties). On the day prior to closing, you should thoroughly inspect the property and obtain a certified check for the funds required, if any, at closing.

At the closing, you will sign, or will have signed all paperwork and deliver certified funds to the lawyer or title company. You will also obtain items such as keys, the garage door opener, warranties, a list of all maintenance and service contracts in effect, and leases, if any. Most closing cost allocations are covered by the terms of the contract. Apportionment of closing expenses is determined by statute, the terms of the contract, and traditions that vary from region to region across the country.

Questions

- Why is it important to begin your general preparations for closing as soon as possible after your offer has been accepted? (See page 15-1.)

- What are the four main documents that guide the closing process? (See page 15-1.)

- What is the purpose of the loan commitment/agreement? (See page 15-1.)

- What information is contained in the closing statement? (See page 15-5.)

- What are six things that you should do during the week before the closing? (See page 15-9.)

- What two things should you do the day before the closing? (See page 15-10.)

- What items should you obtain at the closing? (See 15-10.)

ACTION STEPS

The time you need to prepare for a closing can be shortened considerably if you identify certain resources in advance.

1. Identify two local title insurance companies whom you would consider using for a real estate closing.

2. Look into three insurance companies and select one you might use to handle your property insurance.

3. Contact two local real estate lawyers and interview them to determine which you might use for a real estate closing.

notes:

FINAL COMMENTS

Oftentimes, the real estate closing is the culmination of three transactions—the transaction between the buyer and seller, the mortgage loan between the buyer and mortgagee, and the sales commission between the seller and the sales agent. With so many transactions going on all at once, the first closing can seem overwhelming. But if you take time to attend to the important details in the days and weeks leading up to the closing, your closing will go smoothly, and you'll have taken an important step in your real estate investment career. In fact, after just a few closings, you'll probably start to feel very comfortable handling the details. And who knows—you might even start to enjoy it!

NOTES

NOTES